MAPLE, SUGARIN'

IN VERMONT

A balanced cauldron kettle rose above the fire as evaporating sap lightened it. Stereopticon. *Courtesy of Special Collections, Bailey-Howe Library, University of Vermont.*

Stereopticon view of a primitive sugar camp. *Courtesy of Special Collections, Bailey-Howe Library, University of Vermont.*

MAPLE, SUGARIN'

IN VERMONT

A Sweet History

BETTY ANN LOCKHART

Charleston · London

THE
History
PRESS

Published by The History Press
Charleston, SC 29403
www.historypress.net

All images courtesy of Don Lockhart unless otherwise noted.

Items photographed belong to the Perceptions Private Collection unless otherwise noted.

First published 2008

Manufactured in the United States

ISBN 978.1.59629.491.2

Library of Congress Cataloging-in-Publication Data

Lockhart, Betty Ann.
Maple sugarin' in Vermont : a sweet history / Betty Ann Lockhart ; photos and editorial assistance by Don Lockhart.
p. cm.
Includes bibliographical references.
ISBN 978-1-59629-491-2
1. Maple sugar--Vermont--History. 2. Maple sugar industry--Vermont--History. I. Lockhart, Don. II. Title.
TP395.L63 2008
664'.13209743--dc22
                                   2008030341

To the memory of Dr. Mariafranca Morselli, Dr. Fred Taylor, Fred Laing, Ray Foulds and Sumner Williams—whose avid interest sparked the Vermont Maple History Committee, and contributed to this book. "Old Sugarmakers Never Die—They Just Evaporate."

And thanks to two Vermont "kids" who gathered sap

—

Donald Campbell Lockhart and Elisabeth Marianne Lockhart

—

And to my husband, Don Lockhart, for his great contributions to this book.

Contents

CONTENTS

CONTENTS

Foreword

There is no other product that is as synonymous with the culture and heritage of Vermont than maple. Its rich history dates back to the 1600s and is a keen part of the sense of what makes Vermont unique. Its history and legacy have impacted Vermont in many ways and the maple industry is a very important contributor to our economy.

Maple Sugarin' in Vermont: A Sweet History is a wonderful compilation of the history of maple in Vermont. It covers so many different aspects of how the industry has grown and changed over the years. Also included are some little-known facts about maple in Vermont that might otherwise have remained buried. I hope you enjoy this comprehensive publication that so well details the Vermont maple industry and the important contributions made to our state over the years.

Roger Allbee, Secretary
Vermont Agency of Agriculture

Acknowledgements

Many thanks to:
People whose enthusiasm for a maple history project led them to search memories, review materials, answer questions or mine archives for lost maple facts: Don Harlow; Carolyn Perley; Gordon Goss; Bruce Martell; Wilson "Bill" Clark; George Cook; Larry Myott; Fred Wiseman; Burr Morse; Harold Howrigan; Henry Marckres; Gary Gaudette; Lucien Paquette; John Moody; Bill and Marie Danforth; Mark Isselhardt; Jane Lendway; Karen Fortin; and Emma Lou Craig.

Sugarmaker friends who taught us about Vermont Maple: Sam Cutting III; David Marvin; Robert Howrigan; Everett and Dorothy Willard; Truman Young; Brian Stowe; Cecile and Tom Branon; Ann and Doug Rose; and all those to whom this book is dedicated.

Friends and organizations who permitted the use of maple images, materials and stories that enriched the book: Mary G. Lighthall; Dahlov Ipcar; the von Trapp family; the Vermont Agency of Agriculture; the University of Vermont Special Collections; Harold John Howrigan; the New England Maple Museum; the Abenaki Tribal Museum; the Morse Farm, Whitingham; Donna and Tom Olsen; Grace Brigham; Rick and Diane Marsh; Glenn and Ruth Goodrich; Eugenia Bonyun; Marjorie Palmer (deceased); Christine "Cookie" Barratt; Giovanna Peebles; Andrew Baker; Helen Nearing (deceased); Francis Whitcomb; Joe Packard (deceased) and Emily

Packard; Margaret MacArthur (deceased); Phillippe Beaudry; Joe Roy; Beverly and Hal Frost; Harriet Fletcher-Fisher; Paula Fives-Taylor; Ingrid Bower; April St. Francis; Robert and Mary Coombs (deceased); Dayton and Virginia Fleury; Truman Young; and Bill Godfrey (deceased).

Thanks to Dr. Zacharie and Cynthia Clements, and any contributor who may have escaped this list. Please know how much I appreciate the help of all who enriched *Maple Sugarin' in Vermont: A Sweet History*.

Introduction

> When anybody says maple most everybody thinks of
> Vermont and I think that's not just because Vermont
> makes the most maple syrup. I think it's because of
> the quality of the syrup we produce. In the Green
> Mountain State Pure Vermont Maple is a Proud
> Tradition.
> — *Everett Willard, "Mr. Maple," Vermont Department of*
> *Agriculture, Maple Specialist, retired*[1]

Maple syrup has been made for centuries throughout most of the
region that is now known as Northeastern North America and
southeastern Canada, from the east coast westward to about the
Mississippi River. It is in Vermont, however, that the tradition of
making maple syrup has taken root most passionately. And it is only
in Vermont that our maple syrup has become so indelibly branded
that it is synonymous in the minds of many with the image of the
Green Mountain State. It's an image of hardworking men and
women, of family enterprise, of pristine forests, lofty mountains
clad with pine, birch, spruce and abundant *maples*—sugar maples,
or hard rock maples—*Acer saccharum*!

The image is of purity, freshness and, most specially, flavor. Of
oxen, horses, sledges and deep snow. Of fragrant steam rising from
picturesque sugarhouses. Of sweet celebrations. Of a tradition that
has been handed down from generation to generation to generation.

Throughout the years, Vermont sugarmakers have usually made the most maple syrup in the United States—indeed, for a period of time, more than our neighbors to the north. The latter is no longer true because the Canadian maple lands are vast, and their production area includes the Provincial Lands. However, sugaring in Vermont remains vibrant, progressing from the time of the Native Peoples who first inhabited the land and made syrup in springtime camps to an industry that annually produces in a "good" year more than 500,000 gallons to meet the worldwide desire for the flavor and exceptionally high quality of *Vermont Gold*.

What makes Vermont syrup so special? Ask the sugarmakers! Their answers might be: "It's the natural resource, our sugar maples." "The soils in Vermont are superior for producing sweet sap—there's a difference." "We have mandatory grading laws to protect the quality of syrup we market." "It's the sugarmaking skills that are our heritage."

A stately sugar maple at Shelburne Farms.

Regrettably, our family will never be "Vermonters." That name is reserved for folks who are born here. (Some say to be a Vermonter you must have "one generation in the ground.") However, we have adopted this state, and have become connected to its maple sugaring community and legacy since the time we were asked to produce the first of the three video presentations we have made for Vermont sugarmakers. As we created the videos, we were taught the lore and legend of Vermont maple; we became steeped in the traditions, the products and the history. We traveled to sugarhouses in every corner of the state and collected narratives and oral histories; most special of all, we met genuinely fine, diligent people dedicated to Vermont maple, gracious in welcoming us and willing to share knowledge of Vermont's legacy—folks whom we now count as friends. This book is a look back at the legacy as it has been told to us and as we have discovered in searches of treasure troves in archives, libraries, museums and sugarhouses around the state. In many cases, original documents have been available, sometimes challenging to read, but always making the subject *real*. Some of the documents with their quaint wording are included verbatim so you may experience the romance of the language of the seventeenth, eighteenth, nineteenth and early twentieth centuries. This is a *glimpse*, not a complete history of the Vermont maple industry, but hopefully enough of a glimpse for you to sample the flavor of the Green Mountain State's first agricultural "specialty product." So come along for a trip through "Maple Time in Vermont" from the 1600s through 1950.

Author's Note

The chapter about the Native Peoples of the Dawnland is an exploration of a cultural lifestyle practice that occurred and evolved over time, rather than a single historical event. Much of what has been passed down is not written, or is what might be termed "prehistory." The information presented is a best effort at research, reconstruction and compilation from available sources, some of them original. It is hoped, at the very least, that the reader will gain an appreciation for the Abenaki contribution to our current-day enjoyment of Vermont maple syrup.

The loan of rare, old materials by the Vermont Agency of Agriculture, the New England Maple Museum, Mary Lighthall, Harriet Fletcher-Fisher and Don Harlow greatly enriched many chapters of the book. They provided an opportunity to share with you fascinating insights to the centuries-old history of Vermont maple, and the authentic words of those who "set pen to paper."[2]

Chapter 1

The Native Peoples of the Dawnland—the Abenaki

The Maple is also a good wood...That tree has sap different from that of all the others. There is made from it a beverage very plesing to drink, of the colour of Spanish wine but not so good. It has a sweetness which renders it of very good taste; it does not inconvenience the stomach...This is the drink of the Indians, and even of the French, who are fond of it.
— Nicholas Denys, 1672[3]

My personal feeling is that the Indians were so attuned to the world in which they lived that they were probably far ahead of our beliefs.
— Dr. Fred H. Taylor, professor of botany, University of Vermont (deceased)[4]

The Lands of the Vermont Abenaki

Long, long before there was a place defined as Vermont, there were Native Peoples living in this region, in tune with nature, existing off the land, making temporary and permanent settlements here. They were the Abenaki. The homelands of the Abenaki ranged throughout most of northern New England, including Vermont, northward into the southern Canadian Maritimes. The name given the homeland was *N'da-kinna*, meaning "our land." The Abenaki were divided into two areas—the Eastern Abenaki were concentrated in the area that is now Maine, east of the White Mountains, while the Western Abenaki lived west of the mountains across what is now Vermont and New Hampshire. The southern boundaries of the Abenaki homeland were near the present northern border of Massachusetts.[5] The Abenaki called themselves *Wobanikiiak*, meaning "Peoples of the Dawnland"[6]—Abenaki is the English version of *Wobanikiiak*. The Abenaki Tribal Museum in Swanton Vermont has signage that says "Wobanakik—Land of the Dawn."[7]

The Dawnland Peoples of Vermont are considered by linguists to have been part of the *Alnobak*, or Western Abenaki, and Vermont is one area of the broader lands of *N'da-kinna*. Traditional boundaries, when referring to today's Vermont, encompass the land west of the Connecticut River, to the eastern shores of Lake Champlain, the lake called by the Abenaki *Bitwbagok*. The southern boundaries of today's Vermont Abenaki homelands are in the area where southern Vermont meets the northern border of Massachusetts, and the northern boundaries are in the vicinity of Lake Champlain's

Map of the Abenaki Eastern and Western territories. *Courtesy of the Abenaki Tribal Museum, Swanton.*

The Native Peoples of the Dawnland—the Abenaki

Missisquoi Bay and the Richlieu River. Fred Wiseman tells more about current-day Abenaki Peoples:

> *Three Abenaki communities continue to live in N'da-kinna—the Missisquoi, the Cowass and the Sokoki Abenaki. The Missisquoi Abenaki, the major Native American group in Vermont, is concentrated in Swanton and Highgate in the lower Missisquoi River valley, the heart of a several-thousand-year-old settlement of Abenaki Peoples and the site of an historic village that continues to be a scene of Abenaki communal activity.*[8]

The Native People's name for Missisquoi was *Mazipskoik*.[9]

ABENAKI MAPLE FARMERS

Authors William Haviland and Marjory Power relate that the Western Abenaki "did more farming than did the easterners, who, for their part, devoted more attention to coastal resources."[10] The first crop of the year for an Abanaki farmer would likely have been maple. Regarding maple sugaring, Haviland and Power continue: "As the milder weather of spring approached, subsistence activities shifted back to the villages [in March and April, at the end of winter hunting]. Here, the women and children tapped the maple trees. To do this, a diagonal slash was made on the tree, into which was inserted a hollow elderberry twig." Other reports indicate that a V-shaped slit was made in the tree, then a thin piece of bark was wedged into the V. The sap dripped down the piece of bark into a wooden log with the center hollowed out to form a reservoir. A way of life of the Native Peoples is described that was organized and productive, with seasonal traditions that followed the rhythms of the natural world.

How would the Native Peoples collect the sap? Vessels to collect the sap were part of the Abenaki culture. According to Keith Wilbur, "although birch bark was most widely used, elm, chestnut, basswood, ash, cedar, fir and spruce bark could also be stripped from the tree."[11] Wilbur quoted from John Josslyn's writing in the

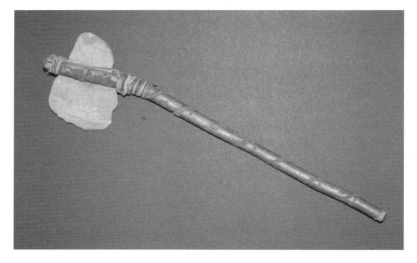

Native Peoples used a tomahawk to tap trees. The illustrations in this book were rendered before recent research, which suggests that, in addition to furs and skins, the Abenaki likely wore colorful cloths obtained through trade with Europeans, as described by Daniel Gookin in a 1654 journal. Querying scholars about how survival would have been possible in the scanty coverings often depicted, the answer was "likely bear grease." When people are active and well-nourished, they are able to tolerate far colder temperatures than commonly believed.

1675 *Account of Two Voyages to New England*: "Delicate sweet dishes too they make of Birch-Bark sowed with threads drawn from Spruse or white Cedar-Roots" To collect the sap, larger pails were made, according to Daniel Gookin, who wrote, in the 1674 account, *Of the Indians of New England*: "Their pails to fetch their water in are made of birch barks, artificially doubled up, that hath four corners and a handle in the midst. Some of these will hold two or three gallons and they will make one of them in an hour's time."[12]

A later description of how birch bark continued to be used by Native Peoples in the making of sap containers was made by W.J. Hoffman in 1896: "The construction of sap buckets, also fashioned from birchbark, cut and folded at the corners so as to avoid breaking and consequent leakage. The folds were also seamed with pine resin…The folds at the top of the rim were held in place by means of a thin strip of wood neatly stitched with strands of basswood bark, and an additional cord

The Native Peoples of the Dawnland—the Abenaki

A Native person collecting sap, painted by Grace Brigham. *Courtesy of the New England Maple Museum.*

was made to extend across the top to serve as a handle."[13] Although this comment was written in 1896, it likely describes basket making that had been handed down from earlier times.

Cold sap is refreshing to drink, but it consists mostly of water. In order to have syrup or sugar (called *sokaal* by the Abenakis)[14], the water must be evaporated. The Native Peoples used several methods to remove the water from sap. It is likely that the people of this region used all of these methods, depending on the time in history, materials they had available, their custom, the areas where they were located and their usual method of cooking. The first, and the method that is actually most often replicated today, involves the use of a large gourd, stump, birch-bark basket or hollowed-out log. Sap was poured into the vessel, stones of a manageable size were heated to a high degree over a fire and then lifted with branches or forked sticks and carried to the fire, where they were added to the liquid. (Caution: We have been told by a person knowledgeable about this practice that there are certain "Grandfather Stones" chosen by the Abenaki for heating; the wrong stones may explode and cause injury!) As the stones cooled, they were removed and

Finely made Abenaki basket, probably Eastern, circa late 1800s. *Courtesy of Vermont State Archaeologist Giovanna Peebles.*

replaced with more hot stones from the fire. The sap heated and eventually boiled. While creating a recent replication in Highgate Center, Native people were told by a tribal elder that covering the bottom of the basket with clay was necessary for a successful boiling in a birch-bark container using "Grandfather Stones" to avoid burning the basket.[15]

The same was true of the pottery containers that, over time, would become brittle and prone to breakage. The syrup resulting from boiling with hot rocks either in birch-bark baskets or in pottery was dark, strong and flavored by the ashes and natural debris that had made their way into the product. Nevertheless it was sweet, and would have been a welcome treat!

Another method involved boiling the sap above the fire in pottery or birch-bark containers. Haviland and Power write that "birchbark pails collected the sap, which was processed by boiling in containers of both pottery and birchbark."[16] Records indicate that the birch-bark vessels were sometimes suspended by grapevines which, when exposed to the fire, were constantly kept covered by moist clay to avoid drying the vines and spilling the sap.[17] Would the birch-bark containers have caught fire? School science experiments prove that water can be boiled in a paper cup, and the cup will not burn below the level of the water in the cup. To boil sap by this method, the Native Peoples would have found it necessary to carefully attend to the fire and the bark containers, frequently filling the containers

Native people boiling sap, painted by Grace Brigham. *Courtesy of the New England Maple Museum.*

with sap. The bark containers were wider at the bottom than at the top, so the heat from under the container would not easily reach above the level of the liquid.

In a note to me, Fred Taylor wrote: "Many northern Indian tribes boiled liquid in birch bark vessels, just as southern Indians sometimes used woven baskets. Neither will burn if the fire does not reach above the liquid level. The known evidence of widespread trade between tribes, often at great distances, would probably disseminate these methods."[18]

A third recorded way of evaporating the sap involves freezing it and removing the ice, which consists mostly of water, with little or no sugar content. Allowing the sap to freeze (usually overnight) and discarding the resulting ice block leaves a liquid with greater sugar content. Successive removal of frozen water results in maple syrup, which, according to Harmon Morse in 1890, "leaves the finest syrup ever tasted."[19] To this day, those sugarmakers who continue to collect sap with buckets toss away the ice before pouring the sap into their gathering tanks, knowing they are concentrating the sugar, lessening the time it will take to boil to the density of maple syrup.

Pottery cooking pot for boiling sap. *Courtesy of the Abenaki Tribal Museum.*

To make maple *sugar* from maple syrup, even more water needs to be evaporated. Frances Densmore described the process in the early part of the twentieth century: "A maple wood paddle was used in stirring the sirup with the back of the granulating ladle, or in some instances pulverized by hand. This had to be done very rapidly before the sugar cooled too much. The stirring of the thick sirup and the granulating was a heavy task, and it was not unusual for men to assist in the work. From the granulating trough the warm sugar was poured into makuks."[20] (Makuks are birch-bark containers, also sometimes spelled makaks, mokuks or mowkuks.) The sugar was also poured into bark cones, or into fanciful molds, designs carved into slabs of wood.

The Legends of Woksis, Manabohozo and Gluskabe

How did the Native Peoples learn about the sweetness of the sap of the maple tree? Two popular legends are told and retold. The story that has been read and heard most frequently was related in a version by Rowland E. Robinson of Rokeby (now Rokeby Museum) in North Ferrisburgh, Vermont. Many variations of the legend exist in publications—this is one of the oldest written references to the legend. Some of the terminology used is considered offensive

The Native Peoples of the Dawnland—the Abenaki

Native Peoples used hot rocks to boil sap into syrup in birch-bark baskets. Reenacted at Carman Brook Farm, Highgate.

to Native Peoples of today—apologies for any offensive reference made in 1896:

> *The true story of the discovery of maple-sugar making is in the legend of Woksis, the mighty hunter. Going forth one morning to the chase, he bade Moqua, the squaw of his bosom, have a choice cut of moose meat boiled for him when he should return…she hawed off the desired tidbit with her sharpest stone knife, and filling her best kokh with clean snow for melting, hung it over the fire. Then she sat down on a bearskin, and began embroidering a pair of moccasins with variously dyed porcupine quills…She became so absorbed in the work that the kokh was forgotten, till the bark cord that suspended it was burned off, and it spilled its contents on the fire with a startling, quenching, scattering explosion that filled the wigwam with steam and smoke. She lifted the overturned vessel from the embers and ashes…and when it was cool enough to handle, she repaired it with a new bail of bark, and the kokh was ready for service again…Happily, she bethought her of the great maple behind the wigwam, tapped*

Native woman making maple candy in a "tree slice" mold, painted by Grace Brigham. *Courtesy of the New England Maple Museum.*

merely for the provision of a pleasant drink, but the sweet water might serve a better purpose now. So she filled the kokh with sap, and hung it over the mended fire...it presently began to boil, whereupon she popped the ample ration of moose meat into it... Then she resumed her embroidery...the kokh boiled low...and lo, the once juicy piece of meat was a shriveled morsel in the midst of a gummy dark brown substance!

She snatched the kokh...from the fire, and then, hearing her husband coming, she ran and hid herself in the nearest thicket of evergreens...aware of an unaccountable silence, she ventured forth and peeped into the wigwam. Woksis sat by the fire eating with his fingers from the kokh, while his face shone with an expression of supreme content and enjoyment. With wonder she watched him devour the last morsel..."O woman of women!...Let me embrace thee!" he cried, and upon his lips she tasted the first maple sugar...The discovery was made public, and kokhs of sap were presently boiling in every wigwam.[21]

The Legend of Woksis, painted by Grace Brigham. *Courtesy of the New England Maple Museum.*

In *Keepers of the Earth*, Michael Caduto and Joseph Bruchac relate the legend of Manabohozo, which is similar to the story of Gluskabe.[22] In the Gluskabe version, possibly not Abenaki but told in Vermont, the magical figure diluted the syrup that once flowed from the broken branches of trees into the mouths of the people, who became fat and lazy. Gluskabe poured water into the trees for thirty days of a "moonth" until the liquid became one thirtieth as sweet. Thereafter the people needed to work hard to have the maple syrup they craved.

Fanciful legends are indications of the long-existing presence of maple syrup in the Native People's culture, when one considers that a legend is a story that has lasted over time. They also illustrate the connection of the Native Peoples to the natural world.

Scholars Argue: Did the Native Peoples Teach the European Newcomers, or Did the Europeans Teach the Native Peoples?

Vermont sugarmakers and botanists have firm beliefs about how the sweetness of maple sap was discovered thousands of years ago. There are some anthropologists who have insisted that the Native Peoples did not have knowledge of the sweet sap nor had the ability to make maple syrup prior to the arrival of the Europeans.

Don Harlow, a sugarmaker from Putney, Vermont, responds:

> *Nonsense! Anyone who's spent time in these woods in sugaring season knows that icicles form where winter storms have broken branches in the maples. Ask any kid who's tasted one of these and you have your answer: they taste wonderful, especially if you haven't been getting a lot of sweets and you're thirsty.*[23]

In a personal note, Fred Taylor wrote: "A few points to consider when looking at legends. Anyone very near maples year-round will have noticed icicles from broken branches or other wounds.

A "sapsicle" is formed as sap drips from a branch while freezing.

Normal curiosity or a need for a drink leads to putting the sap icicle in your mouth. From there, or even from tasting the liquid drops, an association with sweetness comes about." Dr. Taylor firmly believed that the Native Peoples in what is now Vermont knew about maple sugar, had used it as one of their foods and had celebrated its gift long before the arrival of settlers from Europe. Missisquoi Abenakis today like to drink the raw sap as a "spring tonic."

The question of what Native Peoples, in particular the Abenaki, would have been making from the sap of the maple tree "pre-contact"—before European arrival, and before historic records—has been a matter of hot debate among anthropologists. On one side, there is the theory that prior to contact, the Native Peoples could have produced maple syrup, but the high heat required to make maple sugar would not have been possible, considering the limitations of their cooking tools of bark, troughs and pottery. Others, as mentioned, theorize that Native Peoples had *no knowledge* of maple sap or syrup production at all!

In the *Journal of Ethnobiology*, Patrick J. Munson concludes: "For almost 300 years there has been controversy over the question of whether the manufacture of maple products in eastern North America had an aboriginal/prehistoric or European (inspired) historic origin."[24] Munson makes a case for maple syrup, not maple sugar, being made prior to the availability of the settler's kettle.

Arguing to the contrary, there is another possibility. Knowing that maple *syrup* was achievable, might not the Native Peoples have found a way, possibly by evaporation, to produce *sugar* that could be useful to them throughout the year, transportable on journeys and from camp to village? The discovery would likely have been accidental—thicker-than-usual syrup stirred and left in a makak exposed to the air. We will never know because the answer is in pre-history. But if one happens to permit a dribble of maple syrup to remain on a jug or a syrup pitcher after use, evaporation takes place in the refrigerator, eventually turning the dribble into a long, crunchy drip—a hard consistency that is essentially maple sugar!

The availability of kettles, after the arrival of the Europeans, vastly simplified the Native People's work of evaporating maple sap.

From the beginnings of the fur trade, the cauldron or kettle was an item of desire. The lighter-weight copper and brass kettles could be nested, and more easily transported for trade, but iron kettles were also traded. The Vermont Abenaki community of today maintains a Tribal Museum in Swanton, where visitors can see artifacts and replications of Abenaki life. One of the displays is titled, "Maple Syrup Collecting in Vermont and Quebec Abenaki, Nineteenth Century." The display offers the following description:

> *In the spring time the Abenaki would often go to their maple camps to tap and process the maple sap. After the addition of the brace and bit [auger] to the Abenaki tool kit, the trees were tapped and a spile [spout] of sumac with the pith cut out was*

An authentic Native birch-bark sap-collecting basket. *Courtesy of the Abenaki Tribal Museum.*

driven into the hole. The sap would flow out of the hole, down the groove and into the waiting bark collecting basket. One type hung suspended from the spile while the other sat on the ground. From here the sap would be boiled in pottery [early] and poured into bark cone molds to crystallize as maple sugar. It could then be stored for later use.

How the Native Peoples Made Use of the Sap of the Maple Tree

The many ways in which the Native Peoples used maple indicate the significance it held for them. References to primitive use were found by Helen and Scott Nearing and others. Although those references were "post-contact," they likely hark back to earlier times. As the French traders and missionaries interacted with the Native Peoples, they recorded observations that help us to "peep back" in time. The maple tree was of critical importance to survival in some cases!

Perhaps the most important use was for subsistence, satisfying both hunger and thirst: "If they [the Indians] are pressed by thirst, they get juice from trees and distil a sweet and very agreeable liquid which I have tasted several times."[25] Maple was one of several trees from which the Native Peoples distilled sap.

"When in a state of famine, they [the Indians] eat the shavings or bark of a certain tree which they call Michtan, which they split in the Spring to get from it a juice, sweet as honey or as sugar."[26]

"Though, as I have said, we hunted and fished, yet sugar was our principal food during the whole month of April."[27]

"On the mountain, we eat nothing but our sugar, during the whole period. Each man consumed a pound a day, desired no other food, and was visibly nourished by it." The calories supplied by maple sugar energized the workers as they went about the rigorous work of sugaring, producing what they needed for the coming seasons.

Beyond subsistence, records indicate that maple sugar was used as a food, and mixed with other foods—grains, nuts and berries, sweetening and adding flavor—much like maple hot cereal or granola!

"When the savages cooked gruel or mush for us from corn meal they added large lumps of sugar."[28]

"They mix a certain quantity of maple sugar, with an equal quantity of Indian corn, dried and powdered, in its milky state… This mixture is packed in little baskets."[29]

New maple syrup—always a treat! Anyone who has tasted it will appreciate that the Native Peoples, especially children, would be joyful at the time of the Maple Moon, anticipating the first sweet taste!

"The large sugar makak may be always seen there, and when the children are impatient, the mother gives them some of the contents, and they will sit at the door and eat sugar by the handfuls."[30]

"The children and youth carry sap from the trees, and have a grand frolic among themselves, boiling candy and pouring it out on the snow to cool, and gambolling about on the frozen surface with the wildest delight. Their mothers supply them, too, with miniature mokuks, filled with sugar from the first runnings of the sap, which makes the choicest sugar."[31]

"The bark lollipop was filled with maple sugar. Sometimes it was filled with snow and maple syrup poured over it—an early 'ice cream cone,' for the children."[32]

Native children pour thick syrup for sugar-on-snow, painted by Grace Brigham. *Courtesy of the New England Maple Museum.*

cript...yük

Replica of a birch-bark cone made by Christine "Cookie" Barratt, Abenaki basketmaker.

"In making the latter delicacy the sirup was taken from the kettle just before it was ready to grain. It was then poured on snow and not stirred."[33] "Sugar-on-snow," a treat that has survived, remaining popular through the years, and is today still part of celebrations at most fairs, festivals and maple events in Vermont.

"Little cones were made of birch bark…These cones filled with sugar were a favorite delicacy among the children." A larger version of the birch-bark cone was used for sugar storage.[34]

In their wisdom of nature, the Native Peoples used maple syrup as a medicine. Current chemical analyses indicate that in addition to sugars, maple syrup contains amino acids, proteins, organic acids, vitamins and minerals, being particularly high in potassium and calcium.[35]

"They attributed a tonic power to the sap, and in hot weather dissolved the sugar in cold water as a refresher.[36] It [maple sugar] was dissolved in water to make a cooling summer drink, and sometimes made into syrup in which medicine was boiled for children."[37]

Vermonters today frequently choose the Flavor of Vermont—maple syrup, candy, sugar and cream—for their gift giving to

Wooden sugar mold, carved with leaf pattern, typical of that used by Native Peoples.

friends, family and those "from away." Vermont governors and legislators often carry maple gifts when they travel abroad or welcome visiting dignitaries to the Green Mountain State. So it was with the Native Peoples!

"When we reached the villages of the savages we received more than anything else gifts of large pieces of sugar which stood us well in hand on our trip into the wilderness."[38]

"Sugarcakes were made, the molds being cut from soft wood and greased before the sirup was put into them so that they could easily be taken out. These molds were in shape of various animals, also of men, and the moon and stars, originality of design being sought."[39]

"The granulated sugar and sugar cakes were commonly used as gifts."[40]

Native People's Sugaring Camp, by Eugenia Bonyun, from *The Maple Sugaring Story* video.

Sugarin' Country—Where the Maple Moon Beams

The vast area of forested land, lakes and rivers, stretching from the borders of Maine through New Hampshire and Vermont to northern Massachusetts, from Lake Champlain to the Connecticut River, is sugaring country today, where the most maple syrup is produced in the United States. Vermont consistently makes the greatest quantity of maple syrup, and Franklin County, the location of Swanton (the home of the Abenaki Tribal Museum and a seat of Abenaki culture), usually competes for top production records. It must be assumed that the Native Peoples—the *Alnobak* or Abenaki—living in that same region centuries before were wise in the ways of nature, knew the bounty that could be provided by the maple tree when the weather began to warm and used their knowledge to survive and thrive, particularly after the long winter had diminished food supplies.

As this chapter is written, it is the time of the Maple Moon—the full moon when Native Peoples traditionally celebrated the coming of the sugaring season. This is a time of storytelling and traditional dances heralding the flavor and sweetness to come. It is also a time when current-day Vermonters, Native Peoples and others prepare to tap their trees, do the hard work of making Pure Vermont Maple Syrup and launch the season by welcoming visitors to sugarhouses and holding festivals throughout the state that feature maple. It is hoped, at the very least, the reader will remember and appreciate the Abenaki contribution to today's enjoyment of Vermont maple syrup!

Chapter 2

Sugarin' in the Wilderness

Sweetness for the Early Settlers

> *The Emigrants will suffer every inconvenience, privation and hardship; as they advance through the wilderness, they are obliged to prepare a passage by cutting any trees—which might be in the way to impede their sledge or waggon, drawn either, by horses or oxen, the usual way of conveying their children, furniture, Provisions, and &c.*
> — *Wm. Watson, Esq., in* The Emigrant's Guide to the Canadas.[41]

The French explorers and fur traders were among the first Europeans to record the use of sap from the maple trees. Others followed, including groups from Ireland and various parts of the British Isles. Today the Irish and French ancestral influences abound in Franklin County, Vermont. The emigrants benefited from advice offered by Francis A. Evans, Esq., "Late Agent for the Eastern Townships to the Legislature of Lower Canada." Evans noted: "A branch of rural economy and comfort, peculiar to North America, is necessary to be noticed for the information of the emigrant, which is the manufacture of *maple sugar*. The settler should examine his farm, and where he can get from 200 to 500 or more maple trees together, and most convenient, that should be reserved for a *sugary*."[42]

As settlers to "Verd-mont"[43] entered from both Canada to the north and Connecticut and Massachusetts to the south, making their way into the forested wilderness, all experienced similar

Settlers boiling sap, three kettle system, painted by Grace Brigham. *Courtesy of the New England Maple Museum.*

homesteading travails, surviving on the barest necessities. Imagine living on this earliest of the American frontiers! After surviving the bitter cold winter, the first crop that could be harvested was maple syrup, or maple sugar. Written about settling in the Ryegate wilderness in 1774, James Whitelaw's journal noted:

> *When we came here John Hyndman was building his house, so we helped him up with it both for the conveniency of lodging with him till we built one of our own, and also that he might assist us in building ours. Having finished his house, we began to build our own, and had it finished about the beginning of January, 1774. Nothing worth noticing happened till the spring…In the month of April we made about 60 lbs. of sugar, after which we began the surveying of the town.*[44]

The first harvest was maple sap that they boiled to make sugar from their own trees! The story of the first settlers to Danville is a remarkable testimony to the courage of both adults and children on the frontier. Picture the scene as though it were a motion picture drama:

*In 1784, March, Capt. Charles Sias, with his family made the
first actual settlement here. His wife was the first white woman
who dared to breast the long and dreary winter of this deep
unbroken wilderness. Mr. Sias drew his family and effects into
town from Peacham on a hand-sled. Mr. Sias brought with
him 10 children, 7 sons and 3 daughters, as follows: Solomon,
Joseph, Charles, John, Nathan, Samuel, Polly and Abigail.
The snow was very deep, and the way was trackless. No mark
was there to guide them, save the long line of spotted trees leading
away into the forests. The father, with Solomon, Joseph, Charles,
and John and the three daughters made the first company. Sias,
with two men to assist, went forward on snow-shoes, and drew
the load, with the girls and some goods, the boys following.*

*They reached their log cabin early in the afternoon, dug it out
from beneath the snow which had nearly buried it, left John and
the sisters to themselves through the night, and with the others
returned to Peacham. John was but 11 years old...The next
day, came the mother with the other children, on the hand-sled. In
three days more, the effects were all removed, and the lone family
began their hard labors on the wilderness. They commenced
by tapping the maples, which stood thick around them in the
most beautiful groves, affording them sugar in abundance, and
supplied in a great degree, the lack of other food.*[45]

It's late winter. Three men gather around a hearth, discussing
plans to sugar in a place where there is a fine maple grove. Come
spring they will trek through the snow-laden forest, making their
way to Corinth, burdened with sugaring equipment—another
drama to stir the imagination:

*In the spring of 1777, previous to the settlement of the town,
Ezekiel Colby, John Nutting, and John Armand, spent several
weeks here in manufacturing maple sugar. They started together
from Newbury, with each a five-pail kettle on his head, and with
this load they travelled, by a pocket compass, 12 miles through
the wilderness to the place of destination near the centre of the
township.*[46]

One wonders how the three men balanced the kettles on their heads, which, it is estimated, would have been of a size to hold about fifteen gallons, a pail being about three gallons, and how they brought the sugar back to Newbury. Certainly the kettles were of brass rather than the heavier iron!

Confirming the industriousness of the backwoods pioneers, Samuel Williams used the production records in his town of Cavendish to speculate about the amount of sugar produced in Vermont. Williams mentions "families"—indeed, by child-sized equipment that can be found in museums and private collections we know that children were counted on to help with sugaring:

> *We cannot determine with much accuracy what quantity of this sugar is annually made in the state. In the town of Cavendish, in the spring of 1794, the quantity made by eighty-three families, was fourteen thousand and eighty pounds. If the families in the*

Replicated Abenaki and settler spout and trough.

other towns manufacture in the same proportion, there must be above one thousand tons annually made in Vermont.[47]

How that much sugar could have been made in outdoor camps, exposed to wild animals and the storms that frequently arrive at the end of winter and beginning of spring, is mind-boggling. Paintings of the time are all that we have to visually depict sugaring before the invention of the camera. They show either no shelter or, at best, crude three-sided sheds.

"THE OLDEST MAPLE SUGAR ORCHARD IN THE STATE"?

There is a place in Putney, Vermont, close to the southern border of the state, called Kathan Meadows. It is where the Kathan family settled in 1752. The story that has lasted over time is that Captain John Kathan, who, hearing about maple sugar being made by the Native Peoples, sent his young adult son Alexander paddling up the Connecticut River to Putney from their home in Massachusetts to learn about the making of sugar from trees. As Putney sugarmaker Don Harlow relates, if the ice were out of the river enough for Alexander Kathan to navigate the waters, sugaring had to be over for the year. How disappointing! Persistence sent Alexander back again the following year, that time overland and during the sugaring season. Alexander returned home extolling the amount of sugar that could be made from one tree, and the Captain John Kathan family came to settle in Putney.

Ancient trees of the area, evaluated by foresters, have attested to the fact that sugarmaking was done crudely, by slashing trees, either by the Native Peoples with tomahawks or by the early settlers with axes. Huge burls grew about ten feet above the ground, just the right height for wounds that had been made from tapping in deep snow. One of those trees lived on the Harlow farm in Putney until a few years ago (although not alive, it is still standing). When it finally falls, crosswise slices will tell an interesting story. The rings will be counted to determine the age when it died, and the scars made by the long ago taps will tell more of the story. It is said that an account of Alexander's paddling adventure is written in a Kathan Bible. There were two Kathan Bibles—the 1731 Bible of Captain John, and a later one of Alexander's.[48] Captain John's is conserved in the Brattleboro Library. Alexander's Bible left Vermont when a Kathan relative moved to Maine, and its whereabouts are unknown.

Although John Kathan and most of his family remained in the area we now call Putney and Dummerston, the original place name was Fullham (or Fulham). In Benjamin Hall's *History of Eastern Vermont*, John Kathan is mentioned as "possessing the quality of industry and perseverance…did actually clear and improve a hundred and twenty acres, and built a good dwelling-house, barn…and also a saw mill and potash works." In order to guard his improvements, he was "at considerable expense in building a fort round his house and was under the disagreeable necessity of residing therein during the course of a tedious and distressing war."[49] Unless there were maple trees inside the fort, sugar could not have been made during this "confinement to the fort," even though the Kathan family had the necessary potash kettle!

Initially, Alexander Kathan did not remain in Putney. He traveled back to Massachusetts, married, began to raise a family and then returned to Putney. Noted in his Bible was this statement: "I, Alexander Kathan, arrived in Fulham May 1, 1761, with my family from Worcester." Alexander is known to have preserved some forty almanacs, strung on a leather thong, in which he made notes about his business and other affairs. During the 1800s, the almanacs were in the possession of descendants. He wrote about sugaring:

> *March 19, 1764, tapped trees, made 21 lbs. of molasses.*[50]
> *February 1765, tapped trees, and sugred off 18 pounds on the 26th.*
> *Apr. 6, 1778, made off, 10 lbs. of sugar; that's the first this season.*[51]

In a history of the Kathan family, in a section titled, "Alexander Kathan's Maple Sugar Orchard—Oldest in the State," the following is written: "The number of its gigantic old-growth maple trees standing in 1901, is less than thirty, the largest of which measures more than six feet in diameter...In 1858 one of the large maples was cut down and rings of annual growth indicated that nearly a century had passed since it was first 'boxed' for sap to flow in the sugaring season."[52]

Sugaring was part of the everyday lives of most of the settlers. The Kathan records, predating those of others found for this book, are significant because they indicate that Alexander's sugar orchard was likely the earliest-organized lasting maple grove in Vermont, as opposed to other stories that record venturing into the virgin forests to make maple sugar.

WILDERNESS SUGARMAKING: HOW WOULD THE SIAS FAMILY, THE KATHAN FAMILY AND OTHER SETTLERS TO VERMONT MAKE MAPLE SUGAR?

During the settlement years, sugaring was done in much the same way as with the Native Peoples, whom the settlers imitated. However, the Native Peoples had used sharpened stone implements, wooden troughs, paddles, birch-bark vessels and other natural tools. The settlers also made use of the wood available to them from the forests for troughs, dishes, bowls and other household items. The substantial difference introduced to sugaring by the settlers were the kettles, chisels and axes that increased the efficiency of making maple syrup and sugar; indeed, it is recorded that the Native Peoples were anxious to obtain those conveniences and actively traded furs for them. Although they did not originally have the advantage of the metal tools, the Abenaki had the *knowledge* of the trees and the wisdom of the natural maple cycle. On the frontier, each culture shared something important with the other, contributing to the continuation and development of sugaring in Vermont.

Early tapping methods harmed the trees, sometimes killing them. However, the land was often to be cleared for raising crops, and maple trees were abundant, so injuring the trees was not of great concern. An axe cut into the tree about two or three feet from the ground, about two inches deep, in a slash or a V shape. One

Primitive Vermont sugar bowl—one side is for maple and one side is for cane—made from a burl, with a rotating lid.

"Boxing" a tree, an early tapping method. Andrew Baker (sugarmarker, formerly of Charlotte, Vermont) demonstrating boxing in a grove of maples that was to be cleared at Olde Sturbridge Village, Massachusetts.

or two splints of thin wood were fitted into the incision. If the cut were made in an upward direction, it sent the dripping sap in the direction of a trough placed at the bottom of the tree. Troughs were crudely hewn. Every settler planning to make maple sugar spent long winter hours, when there was little else to do, preparing the troughs, cut from logs about two feet long, large enough to contain about two gallons of sap.[53]

Another primitive way of tapping was to cut a "box"—a three-to-four-inch rectangular hole, about an inch or so deep, into the sapwood of the tree. The cut in the bottom side of the box slanted slightly downward into the trunk to create a reservoir where the sap collected. The drips were then conveyed by a splint into a trough below. The sugarmaker went from tree to tree to collect the sap, sometimes straining it through a cloth before boiling.

The final process of producing maple syrup and sugar is called "sugaring off." Earliest records of boiling were of gathering the sap from the troughs and dumping it into a large kettle. A constantly fed fire boiled the sap, and more sap was added as the water boiled away. Adding cold sap to boiling syrup deteriorates the quality of the syrup, but since production was crude on the frontier, quality was not a matter of concern. Later methods of boiling used the "three kettle system." The sap was first boiled in the largest kettle. As it evaporated and became slightly thicker, the liquid was ladled into a mid-size kettle. With further evaporation, the syrupy mixture was ladled into a third, smaller kettle, where it was brought to the consistency of sugar.

One way of determining whether the syrup was boiled enough to become hard maple sugar was accomplished by twisting the end of a vine into a loop, dipping the loop into the boiling mixture and blowing a long "ribbon" through the loop. When a ribbon could be blown that was at least two feet long, the sugarmaker knew the syrup was ready to be removed from the fire, stirred and poured into containers. Another way of determining readiness was to dribble droplets of syrup onto the cold metal of an axe. When it cleaved, or released easily from the axe, it was ready to be stirred and poured into storage containers. If skilled in coopering, the farmer might have wooden pails and tubs for storage. The result was "hard"

Andrew Baker blowing a maple "ribbon" to demonstrate checking for hard sugar readiness.

sugar, sometimes today called "brick" sugar, sufficiently hard so it could be used throughout the year by shaving off slivers or lumps with a chisel or a knife.

VERMONT BECOMES A STATE IN SUGARING SEASON

When the wind's in the North, the sap runs forth.
When the wind's in the East, the sap flows least.
When the wind's in the South, the sap runs droth.
And when the wind's in the West, the sap runs best!
—From an almanac of New England farm songs,
as told by sugarmaker Ed Hamilton to
folk musician Margaret MacArthur

Although the original thirteen states became the United States of America in 1776, Vermont was not among them. Various political issues interfered, and some stalwart Vermonters felt that they would prefer to continue as they were, free to govern themselves. But others, who had previously lived in what was known as the Grants (and then the Republic of Vermont), were in favor of joining the new country. In January of 1791, after negotiating with New York to settle old claims, the assembly convened in Bennington and voted overwhelmingly to ratify the Constitution of the United States. Representatives took the document to Congress, which voted to accept Vermont into the Union. And so it was that on March 4, 1791, Vermont became a member of the United States of America, the fourteenth state and the first to join after the original thirteen.[54]

In Rutland, Vermont, the wind was in the west, and the moon was new on March 4, 1791, as analyzed by Mark Breen of the Fairbanks Museum in St. Johnsbury. During that day, farmers would have been going about the business of tapping maple trees, preparing to boil sap and produce maple sugar. For the first time, they were about to make maple sugar in the *state* of Vermont.

What was the weather like? The answer to that question would have remained a mystery had not Rutland, Vermont, been the home of one of the first detailed weather observers in the United States—the Reverend Samuel Williams, who had settled in the area in 1788 after having been a professor of mathematics and natural history at Harvard University. Williams, who kept a detailed weather diary during 1789, 1790 and 1791, owned a thermometer, barometer and rain gauge. He noted temperatures three times during each day, along with wind, sky and cloud conditions. It is from his original weather diary of late 1790 and early 1791, and some newspaper comments of the time, that it is possible to be in touch with the sugarmakers of 1791 by reconstructing the season.

As winter drew to an end, farmers knew they should be in readiness to make maple sugar. When might serious preparations have begun? By February 17, 1791, the snow in Rutland was five feet deep and there were two more storms that month before the weather began to break. On February 26, the temperatures were +27, +32 and +21 degrees Fahrenheit—warmer, but with a notably "high wind all day,"—not a day when most sugarmakers would have chosen for work in the woods. A better choice would have

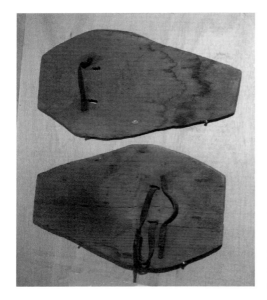

Earliest snowshoes. *Courtesy of the New England Maple Museum.*

been February 27, when temperatures rose to +42 degrees during the day, and winds were light from the west, with sunshine for most of the day. Snowshoes would have been strapped on as workers headed into the woods.

March 4, 1791, dawned clear and sunny. The earliest temperature recording was +22 degrees; by midday the recording was +34, and the last temperature reading recorded was +15. The wind was light from the west all day. Sap may have dripped a little from sun-warmed tapholes in the Rutland area and farther south. Sugarmakers who spent their time preparing on March 4 would have been wonderfully rewarded on March 5. Again, the day dawned clear; the sun, and a light wind from the southwest, remained all day. The early temperature was +8 degrees, but by midday the recording was +49. The sap must have flowed like a sugarmaker's dream—or nightmare, as the struggle began to keep up with the chores of collecting and boiling.[55]

At the end of winter and in early spring, sugarmakers are often asked, "What kind of season is it going to be?" The answer is usually, "Won't know until it's over." The Vermont sugaring season of 1791 has been over for more than two hundred years. What kind of season was it? A sugarmaker with a large grove in the state of Vermont in 1791, not given to overstatement, might have commented, as they do even today: "Made enough for the table, and some left over, if we don't get too much company."

Chapter 3

"T.J." and Vermont Maple

A Mr. Noble has been here, from the country where they are busied with the Sugar-maple tree. He think Mr. Cooper will bring 3000 pounds worth to market this season, and gives the most flattering calculations of what may be done in that way... Sugar...will be no mean addition to the articles of our culture.
— Thomas Jefferson to George Washington, May 1, 1791

Thomas Jefferson was an early promoter of maple sugar. A record of his interest appears in a letter to Benjamin Vaughan on June 27, 1790:

> *Late difficulties in the sugar trade have excited attention to our sugar trees, and it seems fully believed by judicious persons, that we can not only supply our own demand, but make for exportation. I will send you a sample of it if I can find a conveyance without possessing it through the expensive one of the post. What a blessing to substitute a sugar which requires only the labour of children, for that which it is said renders the slavery of the blacks necessary.*[56]

Jefferson approached sugarmaking with tenacity. He availed himself of a copy of a maple sugaring pamphlet. It is a unique privilege to be able to read the words, excerpted from the advice that guided Thomas Jefferson, and consider how they apply to sugaring today—detailed in the following section.

Maple Sugarin' in Vermont

Remarks on the Manufacturing of Maple Sugar

Published by a society of gentlemen, at Philadelphia, for the general information and benefit of the citizens of the United States of America, in July, 1790:

He who enables another to obtain any necessary of life either cheaper or more independently than heretofore, adds a new source of happiness to man;…The transitions, however, made from one stage of improvement to another, are not sudden, but gradual.

That the juice of the sugar maple would produce a saccharine substance answering the purposes of sugar has been known many years, and particularly by the inhabitants of the eastern states; but that there was a sufficient number of this kind of tree in the states of New York and Pennsylvania [Vermont was not a state at this time], *only, to supply the whole United States with this article, is a fact which was not so well ascertained, or so satisfactorily authenticated, till within a year or two past; and that the sugar of this tree was capable of being grained, and produced, in quantity, equal to the best import was in some measure problematical till within even two or three months past, when the arrival of several chests in the city of Philadelphia, made last spring on the Delaware, removed every doubt in the minds of those who have seen it, as to the truth of this last fact…sugar, in colour, grain, and taste, equal, if not superior, in reputation, to any imported…equal to the best sugars imported from the West-India islands.*

The person…whose judgment on this subject is much to be relied on…is clearly of opinion, that four active industrious men, well provided with materials and conveniencies proper for carrying on the business, may turn out, in a common season which lasts from four to six weeks, forty hundred weight of good sugar, that is, ten hundred to each man. If four men can effect this, how great must be the product of the separate or associated labours of the many thousands of people who now inhabit, or may inhabit, the immense tracts of land which abound with the sugar-maple tree!

58

An auger used to tap trees, late 1700s.

Although it has been found that the Sugar Maple Tree will bear much hardship and abuse; yet the chopping notches into it, from year to year, should be foreborne; an auger hole answers the purpose of drawing off the sap equally well, and is no injury to the tree...In all sugar plantations it will be advantageous to cut out the different sorts of timber which grow intermixed with the sugar-maple, which are not thriving, promising trees. The timber so cut out will serve for fuel for the boilers, and leave greater openings for the rays of the sun to enter, which will have a tendency to improve and enrich the remaining trees...Whether this tree is injured or impoverished by repeated tappings, is an inquiry to be expected, and has been frequently made of late...It has been before observed, that it will bear much hardship and abuse, and it may be added, that there are instances...of trees which have been tapped for fifty years or upwards, and continue to yield their sap in the season, equal to any brought into use of later time...How far a careful cultivation of them, the stirring and manuring the soil in which they stand, may improve their value, remains to be ascertained in the future...if it shall thereby

> *be found that these trees can be readily propagated, either from the seed or young plants, and be brought to thrive, so as to be equal in their product, if not superior, to those which have been strewed over the country without the aid of man. To what an extent of cultivation may not this lead! There will be not risk or disadvantage attending the experiment; and it certainly deserves encouragement.* [57]

And so, Jefferson was "encouraged." As his later correspondence indicates, he followed much of this advice and further detailed instructions that were also included in the pamphlet.

PURSUING A MAPLE SUGAR DREAM

In November, 1790, Jefferson purchased fifty pounds of refined maple sugar. It was noted in a record of March, 1791, that Jefferson used the sugar in his coffee. Later, in July, 1791, Benjamin Rush, abolitionist friend of Thomas Jefferson, claimed that Jefferson "uses no other than that which is obtained from the sugar maple tree."

T.J., in a letter sent back to Monticello, dated December 16, 1790, wrote: "I send herewith some seeds…of the Sugar maple… Be so good as to make George prepare a nursery in a proper place and to plant in it…the maple seeds at a proper season. Mr. Lewis must be so good as to have it so inclosed as to keep the horses out." This seed, planted in "the flat ground below the park on the little stream which passes thro' it," failed completely. Comments from botanists and woodsmen indicate two likely causes for the failure: maple seed needs a prolonged period of freezing temperature in order to germinate in the spring; and if the seeds were planted too close to the "little stream," they would not tolerate the wetness.

On May 1, T.J. wrote, "Evidence grows upon us that the U.S. may not only supply themselves sugar for their own consumption but be great exporters."

During a trip to the northeastern states, Jefferson noted in a travel diary on May 27, 1791, the presence of a stand of sugar maples in Cohoes, New York. It was likely the first maple grove that he had seen.

"T.J." and Vermont Maple

Just two months after Vermont became a state, T.J. visited Bennington, Vermont, on June 5, 1791: "Those [botanical objects] either unknown or rare in Virga. were the sugar maple in vast abundance." T.J. spoke with maple sugarmaker Joseph Fay, who agreed to send Jefferson maple seeds in October. Jefferson comments that Fay "had young groves" and intends on planting "an orchard in regular form in the spring." To this day, Bennington County has a lively sugaring community. Since sugar maples can live to be more than two hundred years old, could one of Joseph Fay's saplings, transplanted in 1791, be a grand old Bennington tree?

Possibly spurred on by Joseph Fay's maple orchard plans, on July 6, 1791, T.J. ordered from William Prince, a nurseryman of Flushing in Long Island, New York: "Sugar maples. All you have." Sixty young sugar maple trees reached Monticello about December, 1791, at a cost of one shilling each. The trees were to be planted "below lower Roundabout at North East end in a grove, not in rows."

T.J. corresponded with Joseph Fay on August 30, 1791. The letter was likely a gentle reminder of the promised maple seed. "Every thing seems to tend towards drawing the value of that tree into public notice. The rise in the price of West India sugars, short crops, new embarrassments which may arise in the way of our getting them, will oblige us to try to do without them."

On July 26, 1791, T.J. ordered one hundred pounds of "grained," unrefined maple sugar from New York to send to Monticello. He explained to James Madison: "in order, by proof of its quality, to recommend attention to the tree to my neighbors." According to further correspondence with Madison, the quality of the sugar was poor, and the plan could not be carried out.

Sadly, late in 1792, T.J. wrote: "I am sorry to hear my sugar maples have failed. I shall be able however to get here [in Philadelphia] any number I may desire, as two nurserymen have promised to make provision for me. It is too hopeful an object to be abandoned." Joseph Fay sent T.J. maple seeds on October 8, 1792.

A more hopeful note in Jefferson's "Garden Book," two years later on April 20 in 1794: "There are 8 sugar maples alive."

On March 22, 1798, in a box of plants sent to Monticello were "Sugar maple 2. Plants."

Probably the most quoted Jefferson statement regarding maple sugar urged farmers to be as persistent as he: "I have never seen a reason why every farmer should not have a sugar orchard, as well as an apple orchard. The supply of sugar for his family would require as little ground, and the process of making it as easy as that of cyder."

In November 1809, Jefferson planned a large orchard of "paccans and hickories...to these I shall add the sugar maple if I can procure it. I do not see why we may not have our sugar orchards as well as our cyder orchards."[58]

Although his motives and persistence were admirable, the end results of Thomas Jefferson's visits to Bennington and elsewhere in the northeast, and of all his attempts to establish a maple orchard, were meager. However, some of the trees planted at Monticello *did* survive. One lone sugar maple persisted into the 1980s, but is no longer standing. Thomas Jefferson's contribution to Vermont maple history is the prestige lent by his intense interest in the potential of maple sugar, which has been fulfilled, in part, by Vermonters.

Chapter 4

Flowing Toward the Birth of the Vermont Maple Industry

Winter, which has so long reigned triumphant o'er the conquered year, begins to show indications that his reign is not eternal. The scepter trembles in the old man's hand like a reed shaken in the wind, and he seems to be sensible that he must ere long surrender his authority and retreat before the triumphant advances of the king of day. Every person who has trees should be in readiness to set about the making of maple sugar. This business has been too much neglected of late. Because the imported sugars have been so cheap many farmers have thought it no object to manufacture sugar for themselves. But how I would ask are they to be better employed at this season? The value of that which is imported goes out of the country, and therefore makes it so much poorer.
– *Walton's* Vermont Register *and* Farmers' Almanac, *1836*

VERMONT GEOGRAPHY AFFECTS THE ADOPTION OF SUGARING TECHNOLOGY

The shape of the state of Vermont, and the fact that the southern portion is closer to the population centers of New England, influenced the production of maple sugar. In the north, the state remained less settled, and sugaring methods continued to be more primitive. However, both north and south are reported to have produced large quantities of maple sugar. In 1797, J.A. Graham wrote about sugaring in Bennington County: "The making of sugar from the sap of the maple tree, and of potash and pearlashes, has afforded them with great affluence, at the same time that it tended very much to clear their land." It is known that kettles and augers were being employed in the sugarmaking process; the kettles were also used in the production of potash and pearlash. Samuel Hopkins of Vermont received the first United States patent for making potash and pearlash (potash used in producing soap, glass, and fertilizer; pearlash used as a leavening agent in quick bread).[59] In the spring, the same large kettles were filled with sap! Contrast that with J.A. Graham's 1797 report of making sugar in Caledonia County, in the north, where production was still primitive:

> The season for tapping the Maple Trees, being the time the frost generally leaves the ground, and sap ascends from the roots of the trunk of the tree: of this sap, when drawn off, vast quantities of sugar is made, of a most delicious flavor, but great care is necessary in boiling down the sap, not to let it burn, the method pursued by the Aborigines in making this article was as follows: Large troughs were made out of the Pine tree, sufficient to contain a thousand gallons or upwards; the young Indians collected the sap in these troughs, the women in the mean time (for the men consider everything but war and hunting as beneath their dignity) made large fires for heating the stones necessary for the process; when these were fit for their purpose, they plunged them into the sap in the troughs, and continued the operation till they had boiled the sugar down to the consistence they wished.
>
> There are two kinds of the Maple Tree, from which sap is taken. One, the black, or hard Maple; the other the white, or soft Maple; the former makes infinitely the best grained and best flavored sugar, and fully equal to the quality of the best Mustcavado [cane sugar]. The White Maple most generally grows in swampy grounds, and pores are more open and spongy than the Black Maple.[60]

The wilderness did not remain isolated for long. Settlements grew into towns, and some commerce began. One of the currently used expressions that it is believed to have originated with the maple industry, possibly as early as the early nineteenth century, is "seed money." When the amount of maple sugar produced exceeded family needs, the excess could be sold or bartered, sometimes for seed—just in time for spring planting. The precipitous hills and mountains of Vermont, not suitable for planting, *were* accessible for sugaring. Teams of oxen, and later horses, pulled gathering rigs among the trees as farmers hopped from the sledges to tap the trees, hang the buckets and collect the sap when the weather warmed and the sap began to drip. The animals had an advantage over the tractors that followed many years later, causing some farmers of today to continue to use animals as did their forefathers—the horses and oxen memorize the paths through the woods, and go from tree to tree on their own, with a few shouts of directions from the teamster, a hearty "Ho" or "Come Molly." The farmer can walk along and work in the woods, while the horses wait quietly in place, until the teamster climbs back aboard to head for a more distant grove.

Samuel Williams's 1809 record of the emerging sugaring industry in Vermont provides both descriptions of the nature of sugaring and mention of sugar sale or barter:

> *As the mountains will not fail to supply wood for this manufacture, for centuries yet to come, it seems that Vermont will be one of the states in which this manufacture will be attended with its greatest perfection and profit...The manufacture of maple sugar is also an article of great importance to the state. Perhaps two thirds of the families are engaged in this business in the spring, and they make more sugar than is used among the people. Considerable quantities are carried to the shop keepers; which always find a ready sale, and good pay. The business is now carried on, under the greatest disadvantages: Without proper conveniencies, instruments, or work; solely by the exertions of private families, in the woods, and without any other conveniencies than one or two iron kettles, the largest of which will not hold more than four or five pailfulls. Under all these disadvantages, it is common for a family to make two or three hundred pounds of maple sugar*

in three or four weeks. This manufacture is capable of great improvements. The country abounds with an immense number of the sugar maple trees. The largest of these trees are five and a half or six feet in diameter; and will yield five gallons of sap in one day; and from twelve to fifteen pounds of sugar, during the season. The younger or smaller trees afford sap or juice, in a still greater proportion. Were the workmen furnished with proper apparatus and works, to collect and boil the juice, the quantity of sugar might be increased, during the time of making of it, in almost any proportion: And it might become an article of much importance, in the commerce of the country. I have never tasted any better sugar, than what has been made from the maple, when it has been properly refined; it has a peculiarly rich, salubrious, and pleasant taste. But it is generally made under so many unfavorable circumstances, that it appears for the most part, rough, coarse, and dirty; and frequently burnt, smoaky or greasy, when it is first made. In one circumstance only, does nature seem to have set bounds to this manufacture, and that is with respect to time. It is only during four or five weeks in the spring, that the juice can be collected. While the trees are frozen at night, and thawed in the day, the sap runs plentifully; but as soon as the buds come on, the sap ceases to flow in such as manner, as that it can any longer be collected.[61]

OBSERVATIONS MADE IN 1830

Nathan Hoskins provides an early picture of the emerging Vermont maple industry, helpful in envisioning both the clearing of the land and the concentration of sugaring in the wooded higher elevations. Hoskins mentions a pan and an arch, although it is likely that most sugarmakers were still using kettles:

The manufacture of maple sugar, some years ago, was of very great importance to the state. More than one half of the families in Vermont were engaged in this business, and they manufactured more sugar than was necessary for their consumption. This kind of business is not as much attended to as formerly, except in the towns on the mountain, where large groves of maple trees still remain. In some towns in the southern parts of the state, a second growth of thrifty maples produce large quantities of saccharine juice which is the quality far exceeding that produced by the first growth. Halifax and Guilford in Vermont, and Colrain in Massachusetts, probably make more sugar, in good seasons, than the people require for their consumption. Their groves are mostly of the second growth, on lands which have dropped over or cleared. As soon as the weather is sufficiently warm to the timber in the spring, an incision is made in the tree, either with auger or axe into which a spout is inserted, which conveys the sap to a receiver. From thence it is taken to a place fitted up for boiling, either in the lot or at the house. It is there evaporated in a pan of copper or sheet iron, set in an arch, to the consistency of molasses; then filtered and boiled down to sugar. Two or three hundred weight of sugar can be made with very little trouble or expense from one hundred trees. There is no better sugar than what is made of the maple, and when properly

A Vermont country store tub for storing maple sugar for sale. *Courtesy of the New England Maple Museum.*

*refined has a particularly rich, salubrious and pleasant taste.
The sap runs plentifully while the trees are frozen at night
and thawed through the day. As soon, however, as the buds
start the sap ceases to flow. The quantity of sugar made in
this state has been estimated at 6,000,000 pounds, but this
probably exceeds the real amount.*

Elsewhere, Hoskins observes:

*Vermont has been stripped of her native grandeur...The sugar
maple affording a luxury from its saccharine juices, and great
convenience in its timber and fuel has been so diminished by the
progress of cultivation, that groves of this majestic and valuable
tree once overspreading a large proportion of the State are now
found only on unfeasible, or mountainous lands.*[62]

SUGARING METHODS CHANGE

Transition to newer technologies does not happen everywhere at
once. Thus some of the descriptions recorded list "boxing" of trees
as a method of tapping as late as 1869. Solon Robinson, that year,
in *Facts for Farmers*, admonishes against the practice: "Chopping
great, rough holes into trees to get the sap is as foolish as killing the
goose that laid the golden egg."[63] Though Robinson's warning was
necessary, even as early as 1790, concern for the maple trees was
published in agricultural journals.

Solon Robinson makes two recommendations for crafting
spouts. One, his preferred, is to use "hoop metal" (for coopering
a barrel or bucket) to form small troughs, sharp at one end, which
could be hammered into the tree. Above this handmade spout,
"The right way [to tap] is to bore the trees on the sunny side, two
feet or more above the earth, with an auger not over one inch
diameter, and at first not over half or three fourths of inch into
the wood, with a slant upward. This hole may be deepened or
increased in diameter after the surface becomes so dry that the
flow of sap is checked."[64]

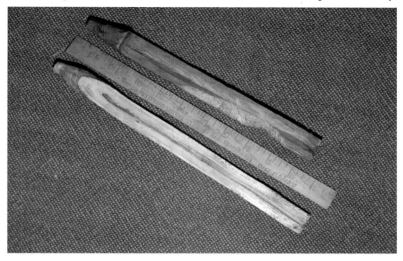

Early sumac spouts, long enough to reach from the tree trunk to a trough below.

A second way used readily available material from the woods: "They [spiles, or spouts] can be made in long winter evenings from elder or sumac which grows on nearly every farm, with no other tools than a saw, a jack-knife, and piece of wire with a handle on one end to remove the pith." An auger, gouge or even a sharp axe made a small hole into which the spout was inserted.

From behind the crumbling plaster walls of our Vermont farmhouse, circa 1810, tumbled two spouts, made exactly as described above. The spouts had been "squirreled away," nibbled by animals who coveted the little bit of sweetness remaining in the wood. The length of these spouts indicates that the farmer living here, Gad Root, had used troughs to collect the sap, the spouts being long enough to reach out twelve inches from the tree to a trough below. Not long after this commercial wooden spouts were manufactured, and available for sale, although most thrifty Vermonters continued to whittle their own.

Sugarmakers who had the tools and were adept at coopering began to make wooden sap buckets to replace the crude, "tippy" troughs that sat on the ground, often contaminated by twigs, leaves and visits from animals. Robinson advised, "Leave one stave long enough to bore a hole to hang upon the nail [wrought]. Do not depend upon things that you can pick up to catch sap, and if you catch a fellow upon your premises making sap-troughs, take a birch sprout and start the sap out of him."

Nevertheless, he mentioned a new, superior advancement—metal sap buckets:

> *The best sap-buckets, and in the end the cheapest, are made of tin, to hold four gallons, and just enough tapering to pack together, with a loop in the rim-wire to hitch up a wrought nail, driven into the tree. Such buckets should not cost over 25 cents each— perhaps not over 20 cents. They should be stored dry, in a dry place, in piles bottom up, and be good for your grandchildren.*[65]

As the population centers grew, farmers in the most developed areas, Connecticut and Massachusetts, found it more practical to sell their maple trees as firewood, and clear the land for crops. Cane sugar was easier to come by, and a more desirable product for the sophisticated tastes of gentry. On the other hand, Howard Russell commented that in "early nineteenth-century western and northern New England towns far from the sources of imported cane sugar, farmers began to produce tons of sugar for sale. Decade by decade, the maple was to be of increasing importance to the hill country."[66]

Chapter 5

Report of the First U.S. Commissioner of Agriculture

Reflecting on the 1700s and Peering into the 1800s

For any domestic purpose for which cane sugar or molasses is used, maple sugar and molasses can be substituted, and in all places where they are to be used in the raw state, I think the maple sugar or sirup is decidedly superior to that of the cane.
— *C.T. Alvord, Wilmington, Vermont, 1862*

The first commissioner of agriculture of the United States, Isaac Newton (not to be confused with Sir Isaac Newton, the scientist of two hundred years earlier) was appointed by Abraham Lincoln in 1862. The post did not become a Cabinet position until 1889. In 1863, a comprehensive report from the commissioner of agriculture was published. The report contained information about U.S. crops, including statistics, history and current methods of production.[67] C.T. Alvord of Wilmington wrote a section which detailed sugaring in southern Vermont in 1862. He also mentioned some new and fascinating facts about early production, and provided insight into the emerging Vermont maple industry.

Alvord described manufacturing advancements and market increases in southern Vermont, indicating greatly improved methods of production, and an industry on the verge of substantial growth. Improvement in tools led to better products, both for the home and for sale, with a corresponding increase in demand, providing a ready market for all that could be made at a time of the year when little else could be done on the farm. He concluded that "there are

Early pottery jug, for storing liquid, including syrup.

probably but a few persons aware of the magnitude and importance of this branch of agriculture in our country." Hopefully, the report raised the awareness of Abraham Lincoln!

Forestry and conservation were concerns mentioned by Alvord. He noted that there was an increase in sugar production between the years 1850 and 1860, indicating that the groves were not becoming extinct. However, he expressed concern for replacement of those trees dying through bad treatment or clearing, and urged farmers to set aside and care for "a few rods of land" to increase the value of the estate and confer "a benefit upon future generations." With the improved production there began to be a concern for the resource, and an awareness of a need to protect and cultivate the sugar maple.

Although it was not until years later that maple syrup replaced maple sugar as the predominant type of maple produced, Alvord was already beginning to notice a developing trend in 1862: "The proportional increase in the quantity of maple molasses manufactured in 1860 over 1850 is much larger than maple sugar… it is thought to be more profitable to make sirup than sugar."

Report of the First U.S. Commissioner of Agriculture

Alvord was highly optimistic about the economic potential of maple. Using the amount of 200,000 pounds produced in Wilmington, he calculated that would be enough to supply each inhabitant with 140 pounds, a supply "for their own consumption and surplus to spare." Alvord indicated that maple sugar had the potential to add to the "wealth of the country…where successfully manufactured is one of the most profitable crops made, and there is probably no branch of the farmer's business that affords as much income and clear profit according to the amount of capital invested and labor expended." Abe Lincoln may have been impressed.

Our knowledge of "the older primitive aboriginal" practices is enriched by the "nuggets" of new facts Alvord added to our information about the earlier history of Vermont maple. "Readying the fire"—preparing a boiling place for using kettles the "old way"—was explained by Alvord. He described cutting two logs, the length determined by the number of kettles used. The logs were placed parallel with a space between them large enough to hang the kettles. "At each end of the logs a notched stick is set into the ground and across these a pole is laid, from which the kettles are hung." As logs were burned, replacements were rolled up.

Gathering has always depended on snowshoes for getting around in the woods—first crude boards, then ash and rawhide. Another item useful for collecting was a shoulder yoke—"made to fit the shoulders of the person who gathered the sap"—from which buckets were hung.

Paintings of the 1860s depict three-sided sheds, with kettles and fires in front. Alvord mentioned that crude shanties were usually erected near the boiling place, and afforded a place for dry wood and tools, to which the boiler could go for shelter from the storm. In some instances, simple structures afforded shelter for sugarmaking right into the twentieth century. According to Alvord, in earlier times during a good run, much sap was wasted because of limited storage—there was no storage available in the sheds.

Filtering began as straining bark and leaves from the sap through rough cloth when it came from the woods. Alvord adds straining the syrup: "Those who wished to make a nice article would strain the sirup through a linen strainer, then clarify it with milk or eggs,

Rawhide-laced snowshoes, lighter weight than the primitive "board" variety.

then strain it again and boil it to sugar. In this way a much better article of sugar was made than one would suppose."

"Done In Done" is an expression from then and now, as is "Happy to see it come, happy to see it go—it's such hard work!" Sugarmakers take care of their equipment at the end of the season, preserving it for the next year. Alvord writes of the days when troughs were used: "At the close of the season the troughs were turned bottom upwards by the tree, or set endwise against it, where they were ready for use next spring. The spouts were taken from the trees, and, with the kettles and other tools, carried to the dwelling-house of the owner for future use."

A major improvement toward cleanliness occurred when buckets replaced troughs. Alvord explains that after some years wooden buckets began to be used in place of troughs, and an auger was used in place of an axe. "The trees were tapped by boring a hole into the tree from one to two inches in depth, and short round spouts driven into the holes; an iron spike was driven into the tree a few inches below the spouts, on which the bucket was hung by means of a hole bored through one of the staves near the top." Sugarmakers still tap about one to two inches into the live white wood beneath the bark.

Sheds were the earliest sugaring shelters; sometimes they were three-sided. Postcard.

Much more is known about the three kettle system than the cauldron kettle "See Saw," an ingenious invention that prevented the syrup from burning if the contents of the pot boiled too low. One of these systems can be seen at the New England Maple Museum and is depicted in the left-facing frontispiece:

> *This large kettle was hung up to one end of a long pole resting on a crotched stick set in the ground; this pole was so balanced that when the kettle was filled with sap, the other end of the pole would rise and let the kettle down to the fire; but when the sap was boiled down low, the kettle would rise out of the way of the fire. The advantage of having it hung in this way was that much less of foreign substances got into the sap while it was boiling; and if the person who was boiling the sap should be absent from the fire for some time, and the sap get low, it would swing up from the fire, and thus prevent it from being burned.*

Prior to the advent of the flat pan evaporator, or simply using what they had to improve on hanging kettles over a fire, some

Wooden bucket and lid, the first improvement after open troughs.

sugarmakers were known to house their kettles in an arch. "Those who had cauldron kettles began to set them in arches made of stone, and these arches were generally protected from the storm by a shelter of some kind," wrote Alvord.

Hauling sap in buckets from the trees to the boiling place was slow, tedious work. Alvord described an improvement—oxen and sledges: "Those persons having sugar lots near their dwelling-houses, accessible to a team, and having conveniences at their dwelling for boiling sap, drew it and boiled it there; the sap was gathered and put in barrels, and drawn on sleds to the boiling place." Sugarmaker labor was still necessary, but oxen bore the load, hastening the job of collecting.

Sugarhouses were a natural next step in the evolution of maple production. What Alvord described in 1862 can still be seen in buildings that pop up here and there in the Vermont countryside. When new sugarhouses are built, they are often similar in design. The slope of a rise in land above the sugarhouse permits gravity to assist in feeding sap into a storage tank in the sugarhouse:

Cauldron kettles set in arches, a transition between the kettle system and evaporators. *From the* 'Cyclopedia of American Agriculture.

Those engaged in the business began to build permanent houses and enlarge their accommodations and facilities for manufacturing…These sugar houses are generally built on the sugar lot, and were made large to contain the boiling fixtures, the storage for sap, the sap buckets when not in use, and generally the wood to be used…The most approved way of building sugar houses now [1862], in this vicinity, is to locate them so that the ground on one side of the house will be several feet higher than on the opposite side. The general plan of the house and fixtures for boiling and storing the sap is as follows: The house is made large enough to enclose the arch. The arch is built near one side of the house, and on the opposite side is built a platform on which the store-tubs are placed. These tubs are so arranged that the sap can be drawn by means of a faucet in the bottom of the tubs into a spout, and run into the heater or pans. On the outside of the building the ground is fitted at such a height that the sap can be drawn from the bottom of the gathering-tubs and run into the tops of the store-tubs. With this arrangement all the labor of

After the first fall of Sugar Snow. Gathering sap with Ox team. Making Maple sugar.

Sugaring with oxen eased the labor. Postcard. *Courtesy of Special Collections, Bailey-Howe Library, University of Vermont.*

> *lifting the sap after it is placed in the gathering-tubs or buckets and brought to the house is avoided; the only force used after this until the sap is in the pans is that of gravitation. In the sides of the building are doors, so calculated as to afford means for the steam from the boiling sap to pass off.*

Later, "cupulas," vents at the top of sugarhouse roofs, allowed rising steam to escape more directly.

Arches and pans added "fuel to the fire," vastly improving boiling efficiency. Arches are the substructures that hold the pans, and in which the fire is built; usually made of brick or stone, they retain heat, similar to an oven.

Alvord explained:

> *The arch is usually made wide enough to set on one pan and long enough to place one or two pans as may be required...The mouth of the arch is fitted with a cast iron frame and door. About eight inches from the bottom of the arch is a bed on which the fire is made: this floor is generally made of narrow, flat stones, with sufficient space between them for the coals and ashes to fall*

Presson R. Gale sugarhouse, circa 1850, was located where the Trapp sugarhouse is today. *Courtesy of the Trapp Family Lodge.*

> *through…In this arrangement of the floor, the draught of air passes under and up through the fire, throwing the flame and heat against the bottom of the pans…The pans for boiling the sap are made of Russia sheet iron, and are of different sizes, holding from one to four barrels…a three-barrel pan, five feet four inches long, three feet three inches wide…The depth of the pans is seven and half inches…Handles are placed on the sides of pans near the top. The cost of the pans will vary with the price of iron and also the quality of the stock.*

Those efficient evaporators! Alvord stated that with clear weather, when sap would boil faster, a sugarmaker with a three-barrel pan and a "heater" could make eighty pounds of sugar in an average day's work! The "heater" was a complicated invention by a Wilmington sugarmaker. As described by Alvord, it passed heat and smoke through tubes below the pan, exposing a larger surface to the action of the fire—an early instance of sugarmaker "tinkering" to speed the boiling process.

Buckets and spouts were a major advancement over the open troughs, which collected water and debris in the sap. Alvord

Interior of an early sugarhouse with a wooden storage tank. Postcard. *Courtesy of Special Collections, Bailey-Howe Library, University of Vermont.*

described the 1862 status of buckets and spouts, which indicate a transitional period from wood to metal, and from home produced to factory made. Antique wooden sap buckets make charming wastebaskets!

> *The buckets used to catch sap are made both of wood and tin, the wooden ones being generally used. These are made of pine lumber, hooped with iron, painted with oil paint on both sides; at the top of the bucket, on the outside is an ear made of sheet iron, through which is a hole large enough for the spike to pass on which it is hung. These buckets are made at factories [as opposed to the first hand-coopered buckets], and cost from ten to twelve dollars a hundred, and will hold about ten quarts each. Tin buckets can be obtained at the tin shops, and will cost from twenty-five to thirty-eight cents each. The spouts used for conveying the sap from the tree to the bucket are principally made of wood, although metallic ones are used to some extent. The wooden spouts are made of hard wood, birch making the best.*

80

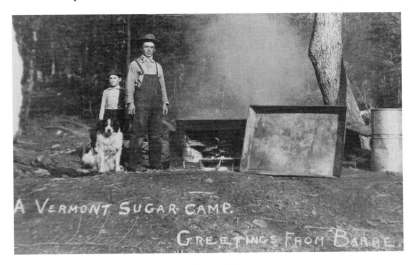

Sugar camp postcard, with an early "flat pan" evaporator.

They are made by taking inch boards, sawing them into strips one inch wide, then cut into pieces the length of the spout, which is about six inches; these are then put into a lathe and turned round smooth, one end of which is tapered down to a little less than half an inch in diameter; a hole about one-fourth of an inch is then bored through the entire length, and the spout is ready for use. These cost thirty-four cents per hundred. The spikes for hanging the bucket on the tree are made of wrought iron, and are about two inches in length, with the head on one side of the nail, to prevent the bucket from slipping off. The present cost is about forty cents per hundred. A common half-inch bit is used for tapping the tree, though many use a seven-sixteenth of an inch for that purpose, and a one-half inch bit for boring the second time [if the first hole should dry out].

Some sap-gathering and storage tanks were round, others were not. The "Tomahawk" gathering rig, oval shaped, was manufactured in Wilmington, Vermont, by Adams and Haynes, beginning about 1850. A Tomahawk is still in use at the Morse Farm in Whitingham, drawn through the woods by an elegant pair of horses, Jesse and

"Collecting Sap" postcard—gathering pails are wider at the base than the top to avoid spillage. *Courtesy of Special Collections, Bailey-Howe Library, University of Vermont.*

Mandy. All gathering tanks in Alvord's time were made of staves, similar to those used in barrels, but larger. The wooden staves of the round gathering rigs were aligned vertically, like a large barrel. The staves of the Tomahawk rig ran lengthwise eight feet and varied in outside diameter from 36 inches to 51 inches.[68]

> *In all sugar lots where the surface of the land will admit of a team being used, the sap is drawn from the different parts of the lot to the sugar house, on sleds, by oxen. For this purpose a gathering-tub, holding three or four barrels, is used. This tub is made…with the diameter of the bottom being much larger than the top to prevent it from tipping when filled. In the top of the tub a hole is cut large enough to turn in the sap; a lid is made to fit this hole, so that when the tub is full it can be closed tight, to prevent the sap from being wasted in going to the house. The tub is fastened on the sled with stakes or chains. The tubs in the house for storing are usually about the size of the gathering-tubs…the tops of these are the largest. Both the gathering and storing tubs are made of spruce or pine boards, hooped with iron, and usually painted on the outside.*

Report of the First U.S. Commissioner of Agriculture

Collecting with wooden buckets (pictured in the foreground), yoke and snowshoes, typical of nineteenth and early twentieth centuries. Postcard. *Courtesy of Special Collections, Bailey-Howe Library, University of Vermont.*

It is little known that a first attempt to carry sap downhill without people or rigs was made when some sugarmakers experimented with wooden tubing! What Alvord calls a "spout" was indeed a narrow, open wooden pipe, constructed in sections, fitted together and then laid on the ground. Thereafter crude metal pipeline began to appear, also laid on the ground:

> *Many of the sugar lots are located on the sides of hills so steep that neither teams nor hand-sleds can be used to draw the sap. In these lots leading spouts can be used in a way to save much severe labor. By having the sugar house located at the lowest part of the lot, lines of leading spouts can be put up to different parts of the lot, and in these spouts the sap can be run from those places to the house. The first kind of spouts used was made of wood in the following manner: Spruce logs were sawed into scantling 2 ½ to 3 inches square, from 14 to 16 feet long; on one side of these sticks a groove was cut sufficiently deep for the sap to run; this groove is cut with a shaving or drawing knife made in the shape required. The ends of the spouts are made so that the end of*

83

Left: Tin gathering pail, smaller at the top than the bottom to reduce splashing.

Below: Collection of wooden and metal spouts, includes the transition from the handcrafted to machine made.

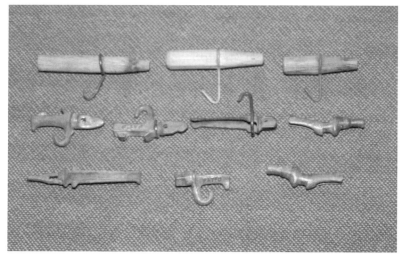

one spout will lap over the other, and are fitted to match so that the sap will not leak at the joints…These spouts cannot be used when it snows, as the snow that falls into them will choke up the passage of the sap, so that it will run over and waste. In rainy weather considerable water will collect in the spouts if the line of spouts is a long one; but by taking advantage of the weather these inconveniences can generally be avoided…The tin leading spout, lately introduced in this vicinity, is a great improvement on the wooden spout. It can be used as well in stormy as in pleasant weather. It is made in the form of a tube or pipe, in lengths of

A team of horses pulling a Tomahawk gathering rig.

eight feet. The size of the tube generally made is one-half inch, and costs thirty-seven cents per rod; one end of these spouts is made a little larger than the other, so that the ends will fit tight in putting them up.

In his 1862 report, Alvord described the production of various kinds of maple sugar, hard and soft—sugar for molds and for bricks. His commentary on "hard sugar" told about the maple product that was used to make sturdy chunks, blocks or shapes from which sugar can be shaved:

The degree of hardness to which the sugar needs to be boiled depends on the subsequent treatment...if it is to be put into cakes...it is necessary to boil it as long as it can and not burn. There are various ways of telling when the sugar is boiled enough...when it will form bubbles, feathers, or ribbons, on being blown, it is done enough to cake or stir. To try it in this way, take a small wire or stick and form one end into a loop; dip this loop into the sugar and blow through it to produce the forms described...Both wooden and tin molds are used to cake sugar

Wooden mold for making hard sugar blocks.

in, and these are made of different forms and sizes—the weight of the cakes varying from two ounces to several pounds.

A sugarmaker code then and now is "Clean and Sweet." Bacteria will multiply quickly in unclean containers, spoiling the sap and any syrup made from it. Hot water and "elbow grease" are the time-honored answers:

In making maple sugar or molasses, one thing is indispensably necessary in order to make a good article; that is, cleanliness in every process from the time the sap is collected till it is made into sugar. Great care should be taken that all implements used to hold the sap or sirop should be kept clean and sweet...Experience has shown that the sooner the sap is converted into sugar after it leaves the tree, the better; and especially is this the case when the weather grows warm...At such time the boiling should be forced to the utmost extent, night and day, if necessary.

Night boiling was frequently a necessity prior to the time of plastic tubing and large, efficient rigs. Rick Marsh, sugarmaker of Jeffersonville, Vermont, tells the story of his grandfather who avoided dozing off during late-night boiling; falling asleep can lead to burning the pan, disastrous to the pan, the syrup and sometimes the sugarhouse. By the side of the evaporator he had a crutch with a seat attached. If Grandpa fell asleep, his seat would tip over, warning him about the impending ruin!

The word *varies* is the important one when considering the following, regarding the sugaring season and sugaring weather! Seasons are recorded that have begun in late April (1798) and as early as late January. What Alvord mentions has been the norm over the years:

> *The time for making sugar* **varies** *with the season. Some years I have known the sugar season to commence the last of February, and in others not till the first of April. The usual time, in this vicinity, is about the 10th of March, and generally lasts about six weeks.*

"Putting sirup by" meant that if syrup were to be safely kept and even shipped away, a dependable, tight container was needed. "Putting syrup by" did not happen reliably until tight wooden, glass, pottery or metal containers were available.

> *Within a few years the manufacturers of maple sugar in this vicinity have been, to some extent, making maple sirup or molasses for sale instead of sugar. Where it can be sold in this form it saves much labor that is required to make it into sugar. The sirup is put into wooden kegs holding several gallons each, and tin cans holding from one to four gallons each. These cans, after they are filled, are sealed up air-tight, so that the sirup will retain its flavor some length of time and they can be safely transported to any part of the country.*

The year 1862 was a time of Civil War. Vermont farm boys left for the southern battlefields, and some did not return. Civil War records tell that Alonzo Root, grandson of Gad Root (the 1862 owner of our farm), was one of the unfortunate Vermonters.

Maple Sugarin' in Vermont

Alonzo died in Fairfax, Virginia, on December 31, 1862—a young sugarmaker far from home. It is known that sugaring happened here—a yoke, spouts and an 1836 almanac connecting sugaring with antislavery sentiments were discovered. Of the Civil War, Alvord wrote:

> *In the present complicated state of our national affairs the manufacture and production of maple sugar is a subject which commends itself to the consideration of every one having the facilities for engaging in this branch of business. The present high prices of sugar if no other consideration was taken into account, are sufficient to induce those engaged in the business to enlarge and extend their operations as far as their means will allow, and also to stimulate others not now engaged in the business to improve those opportunities which they may have of increasing the amount of sugar made, both with profit to themselves and benefit to others.*

Chapter 6

"Eat Sugar Not Made By Slaves!"

Make your own sugar and send not to the Indies for it. Feast not on the toil, pain and misery of the wretched.
— Farmers' Almanac, *1803*

Nor is that all. The use of imported sugar encourages slavery, for nearly all the imported sugar is made by slaves. Let antislavery men then show their opposition to the nefarious traffic in human flesh and blood by the encouragement of the domestic manufacture of maple sugar.
— *Walton's* Vermont Register *and* Farmers' Almanac, *1836*

Although it is known that some slaves were kept in Vermont, there were never many—slaveholders were far more the exception than the rule. In 1777, Vermont was the first territory (it was not a state at that time) to abolish slavery. The first *state* to abolish slavery was Pennsylvania, which followed Vermont's example three years later in 1780. In the nineteenth century, the Green Mountain State was well known for its efforts to assist slaves escaping from the South to the Canadian border, where freedom awaited them. In our home, there is a small hidden room behind a fireplace, accessible by a loose board on the second floor. The story is told that the room was a "hidey hole," in which slaves were safely kept on their way north. Such "hidey holes" are common in this area. Two nearby homes had underground tunnels beneath the road, through which slaves could escape to a building across the way. When masters or bounty hunters arrived at the place where the slaves were hiding, the slaves could use the tunnel to find safe haven across the road, then run back through the tunnel as the master or slave chaser approached the temporary hiding place—a clever ploy that aided the slaves' escape to Canada and freedom. Rokeby Museum in Ferrisburgh, Vermont, six miles south of our farm, is the historic home and farm of the Rowland Robinson family. The home is well documented as a location on the Underground Railroad, where slaves safely stayed in a small upstairs room—at least one of them spent time there, working on the farm. However, according to Jane Williamson, the museum director, only one brief reference indicates that the Robinson family sugared—a complaint in the writings of Rowland Robinson about getting soaked hauling cold sap. Jane surmised that since "everybody sugared," it was taken as a matter of course, and was not something about which the family kept records. Also, when trees were cleared for farming, it is possible that most of the sugar maples were sacrificed, restricting any sugaring operation. The Robinsons were Quakers, and Quakers had long been vigorously opposed to slavery, resulting in their advocacy for the production of maple sugar. It is easy to imagine a slave running the six miles north, along the dirt road or through the woods to Gad Root's farm, to be hidden behind the fireplace. Later, they traveled north, perhaps to one of the Burlington stations on the Underground Railroad, then seventy miles farther to Canada.

By 1837, there were eighty-nine antislavery societies in Vermont, having more than five thousand members. Rowland Robinson was the first chairman for the committee for the Vermont Anti-Slavery Society formed in 1843. The purpose of the organization was to "improve the mental, moral and political condition of the 'colored population' and abolish slavery in the United States." They wished to accomplish their goals by peaceful means, "exposing the guilt of holding men as property." Newspapers and pamphlets were written, distributed and read in churches. Songs and poems were published.[69]

Connecting Vermont Maple Sugarmaking with Antislavery Efforts

Prior to the Civil War, much political activity linked maple sugar with the antislavery movement. Dr. Benjamin Rush, friend of Thomas Jefferson and influential leader in the second Continental Congress, was associated with the Pennsylvania Society for Promoting the Abolition of Slavery. In 1787, Rush and Benjamin Franklin united to lead the society, and wrote and spoke against slavery. Rush, in concert with the Quakers, aimed "to lessen or destroy the consumption of West Indian sugar, and thus indirectly to destroy negro slavery." Urged by Thomas Jefferson, then the Secretary of State of the United States (Jefferson was the first in that position) and president of the American Philosophical Society, Rush prepared a scientific paper about the production and use of maple sugar that he read at a meeting of the Philosophical Society in 1791. He contrasted maple sugar with cane, and stated that compared with sugar made in the West Indies the maple was cleaner:

> It is prepared in a season of the year when not a single insect exists to feast upon it or to mix its excrements with it, before particles of dust can float in it. The same observation cannot be applied to West India sugar. The insects and worms that prey upon it and, of course, mix with it compose a page in a nomenclature of natural history. I shall say nothing of the hands which are employed in making the sugar of the West Indies, while maple sugar is made by persons educated in habits of cleanliness…I cannot help contemplating a sugar maple tree with a species of affection and even veneration, for I have persuaded myself to behold in it the happy means of rendering the commerce and slavery of our African brethren in the sugar islands as unnecessary, as it has always been inhuman and unjust…in contemplating the present and opening prospects in human affairs, I am led to expect that a material part of the general happiness which heaven seems to have prepared for mankind will be derived from the manufacture and general use of maple sugar.[70]

The "Maple Sugar Bubble"

It is not surprising, then, that when Thomas Jefferson journeyed to Vermont and New York later in 1791, his interest in maple sugar was keen. The potential maple sugar had to become a commercial product in the new United States, eliminating dependence on sugar from the British West Indies, tantalized Thomas Jefferson. His enthusiasm was nurtured by Arthur Noble, a land developer of New York State, and Noble's associate, William Cooper, for whom Cooperstown, New York, is named. The two men, joining with abolitionists, had created what has been called the "Maple Sugar Bubble," an unrealistic estimate of the amount of maple sugar that could be produced in family sugar orchards. Profit was at least part of the motive for Cooper and Noble, who used abolition and the sugar maples that were on their lands in Otsego County as a sales point. Attempting to lure purchasers, they termed the sugar maples "these diamonds of America." Jefferson brought this enthusiasm with him when he visited Bennington, Vermont, where he encouraged the farmers there to be more systematic in their approach to sugaring, establishing orchards of sugar maples (as he planned to do at his home in Virginia) rather than merely going into the woods to tap trees. Jefferson's attempts at establishing a maple grove at Monticello are the subject of the third chapter.[71]

As time passed, the Vermont governor and legislature continued to make their opposition to slavery known, becoming more aggressive. Walter Crockett recorded that in 1841 the Vermont legislature adopted a resolution providing "that the Constitution of the United States ought to be amended so as to prevent the existence and maintenance of slavery in any form or manner." A bold step toward advocating abolition![72]

Next, in 1843, Vermont Governor John Mattocks spearheaded a Personal Liberty Bill that provided that "no court of record or any Judge or Magistrate, acting under the authority of the State, hereafter should take cognizance or grant a certificate, warrant or other process to any person claiming any other person as a fugitive slave in the State of Vermont." This bill was squarely aimed at the fugitive slave owners and bounty hunters, providing legal

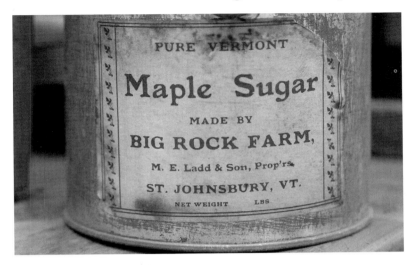

Maple sugar was marketed in "Vermont Maple Sugar" cans.

instructions for the courts. Whether or not any court or judge sympathized with the slave owner, the law was clear—the demands of the slave owner or bounty owner were not to be recognized in Vermont.[73]

The prediction of Benjamin Rush that maple sugar could abolish slavery did not come to fruition, but it was Vermonters who fought vigorously in Congress for abolition of slavery, and whose actions in the Vermont legislature infuriated the Southern states. Although maple sugar did not end slavery, it became the sweetener of choice in homes of the abolitionists and others, not only in the United States but in other parts of the world. It was, in part, the Vermonters who helped slaves to freedom through the Green Mountain State's section of the Underground Railroad, and the sacrifices of the Vermont regiments that were renowned for fighting fiercely in the Civil War, that led to the end of slavery in the United States.

Chapter 7

Heading through the 1800s

"MAPLE SWEET"—THE VERMONT SUGARMAKERS' SONG AND PERRIN BATCHELDER FISKE

"Maple Sweet" was written by Perrin Batchelder Fiske, born in Waitsfield, Vermont, in 1837. Originally, it appeared in a songbook, *The Palm*, and is included in the Helen Hartness Flanders Collection of Vermont folk songs housed at Middlebury College. Margaret MacArthur, Vermont folklorist and folk singer, performed this song on her *Almanac of New England Farm Songs* album.

"Maple Sweet"[74]

When you see the vapor pillar
Link the forest and the sky
Then you know that sugarmaking
Season's drawing nigh.
Frosty night and thawy day,
Make the maple pulses play,
'Til congested by their sweetness
They delight to bleed away.

Chorus:
Then bubble, bubble, bubble, bubble

Bubble goes the pan.
Furnish better music for the season
If you can.
See the golden billows,
Watch their ebb and flow,
Sweetest joys indeed
We sugarmakers know.

When you see the farmer trudging
With his dripping buckets home
Then you know that sugarmaking
Season is past come.
Fragrant odors pour
Through the open cabin door.
The eager children rally
Ever loudly calling "More!"

Illustrations from *One Horse Farm. Courtesy of artist/author Dahlov Ipcar.*

Chorus

You may wax it you may grain it
Fix it any how to eat.
You'll always smack your lips
And say it's very very sweet
For the greenest leaves you see
'Neath the spreading maple tree
They sip and sip all summer
And the autumn beauties be.

Chorus

Oh you say you don't believe it
Take a saucer and a spoon.
Though you're sourer than a lemon

You'll be sweeter very soon.
'Til everyone you meet
At home or on the street
Will have half a mind to bite you
For you look so very sweet.

The Maple Scene in 1873 and E.A. Fiske

In *The Second Report Of The Vermont State Board Of Agriculture, Manufactures And Mining For The Years 1873–1874*, E.A. Fiske of Waitsfield wrote about maple sugar. He was likely related to Perrin Batchelder Fiske, author of "Maple Sweet." E.A. stated that the statistics for 1860 show New York producing 10,816,458 pounds of maple sugar and Vermont producing 9,819,939 pounds. In actuality, however, Vermonters were producing far more per capita because of the size of the state. "If divided equally, Vermont could give to each inhabitant thirty pounds of sugar, while New York could give only about two and one half pounds to each of hers," an indication that sugaring was an industry being avidly pursued in the small state of Vermont, more so than in any other state in the Union—which is true to this day.

When detailing 1873 production methods, Fiske wrote that the public preferred to view maple sugaring as it was done in earlier times:

> *Perhaps there is no branch of farming in which more improvement has been made in the last thirty or forty years than in the manufacture of maple sugar…If the popular writers of the day allude to the subject at all, the reference is invariably to the primitive style of the manufacture, whether it is found in a book, magazine, or newspaper, or a juvenile, and if engravings are introduced to illustrate, they are always of the same character. Whether this is because improvements eliminate the poetry and romance, or because the subject is not considered of sufficient importance to demand a thorough examination, I am unable to say; but let one who has used the modern improvement of the most*

*approved pattern go back to the mode of our fathers…and if he
finds poetry in it, I think he will say, I prefer prose hereafter.*

Sugarmakers of today would sympathize with this. It is difficult
to excite the media about the image of modern tubing and
stainless evaporators, although they are the devices that produce
the quantities of syrup necessary to meet the needs of consumers.
Most sugarmakers nowadays would not be able to manage teams
of horses and the large labor force necessary for collecting sap with
buckets. It is fortunate that some sugarmaking families *do* prefer to
sugar with buckets and horses, can meet the interests of the media
and perpetuate the romance of yesterday.

Fiske enthusiastically described the advantages of the Bellows
Falls evaporator that he had been using for three years, and
although he mentions the wooden "spout" (open pipeline) that
carries sap down the hill, and tin "spouts" or tin pipeline, he
mentions a far more efficient way for sugarmakers to collect sap
from their orchards by means of the "sap gatherer" or "draw tub":
"a hogshead containing from one hundred to one hundred and

Fairfield teamster collecting sap.

99

Left: Inez Abbott sugaring, Cabot, circa 1910. *Courtesy of Goodrich's Maple Farm.*

Below: Inez Abbott, collecting with her team, circa 1910. *Courtesy Goodrich's Maple Farm.*

fifty gallons…By means of oxen or horses and sled and such a tub as this, we have a convenient, portable gathering place, and where trees are greatly scattered this is the only practicable plan."[75]

An especially poignant comment was made by Fiske:

> *The true Vermonter* [and perhaps the true Vermonter at heart!] *never loses his taste for the sweet of the maple. Although in after years his home may be in the great city, or on the prairies of the West…yet year by year, when he knows that it must be*

early spring in the old homestead, his thoughts go back to former days, and he forgets the weariness and toil, the bitter part of his early life, and remembers the sweet alone. Prompted by such thoughts as these, many a letter comes back to the old homes, and many a package of maple in solid or liquid form finds its way from the Green Mountain State to other climes, as a token that dear ones far away have still a place in the heart.

In this age of scattered families, even if a Vermont family is not one of sugarmakers, often the request for a maple "taste of home" is made, and the package of syrup or candy is shipped.

Fiske concluded his 1873–74 musings with: "May it long be the mission of the maples thus to sweeten the cup of life."[76]

Chapter 8

The Auspicious 1890s

THE SUGAR BOUNTY

In 1890, a tariff act was passed by Congress known as the McKinley Bill. The bill had several thrusts, among them an attempt to stimulate the growth of the sugar industry in the United States, including maple sugar. The bill is sometimes mentioned as an illustration of the independence of Vermonters and their ability to analyze a new scheme that might backfire to their disadvantage. The *Twelfth Vermont Agricultural Report by the State Board of Agriculture for the Years 1891–1892* provided the following details to sugarmakers:

SUGAR BOUNTY

In a tariff bill lately passed by Congress occurs a provision giving a bounty on sugar made in the United States. The section reads as follows:

ACT OF OCTOBER 1, 1890
AN ACT TO REDUCE THE REVENUE AND EQUALIZE DUTIES ON IMPORTS, AND FOR OTHER PURPOSES:

SECTION I.
BOUNTY ON SUGAR.

231. That on and after July first, eighteen hundred and ninety-one, and until July first, nineteen hundred and five, there shall be paid, from any moneys in the Treasury not other wise appropriated, under the provisions of section three thousand six hundred and eighty-nine of the Revised Statutes, to the producer of sugar testing not less than ninety degrees by the polariscope, from beets, sorghum, or sugar-cane grown within the United States, or from maple sap produced within the United States, a bounty of two cents per pound; and upon sugar testing less than ninety degrees by the polariscope and not less than eighty degrees, a bounty of one and three-fourths cents per pound, under such rules and regulations as the Commissioner of Internal Revenue, with the approval of the Secretary of the Treasury, shall prescribe.[77]

Maple Sugar Bounty License. *Courtesy of Vermont Maple Outlet.*

The "rules and regulations" were many! They included provisions for "Notices, Application for License, and Bonds," "Licenses" (annual only), "No Bounty to be Paid in Certain Cases," "Regulation and Inspection," "Payment of Bounties," "No Bounty On Less then Five Hundred Pounds," "Penalties" and "Inspection." Bounties were provided for *sugar* only, and to qualify, the sugarmaker had to produce at least five hundred pounds of sugar.

One question in the minds of sugarmakers that year was: "Can we afford to make sugar and get a bounty rather than sell our product in the form of syrup?" Another must have related to the amount of additional labor and wood required to take syrup to the level of sugar. However, applying for the license did not require a commitment to actually produce the product.

The report continues with 1892 statistics that indicate an estimated 10,099 persons in the state in 1889 made five hundred pounds or more of sugar, and therefore would be eligible for the bounty. It was expected that at least one-half of them would apply for the bounty; in fact 2,609 took out license papers—a little more than one-fourth of sugarmakers eligible for the bounty took the first steps necessary to obtain it. Many of the licensed did nothing further; 1,918 actually had sugar weighed and tried for the bounty. The 691 who took out licenses but did not present any sugar to be weighed had various reasons; some did not tap their orchards that spring, some did not make five hundred pounds, some made syrup instead of sugar and many were misled by the warm spell that occurred in the middle of the sugar season, thinking that sugaring was over and, as they had not made five hundred pounds at that time, sold what they had without having it weighed. Of the 1,918 who tried for the bounty, 1,671 succeeded and 247 failed—the latter divided into 68 who failed because they made less than five hundred pounds, and 179 because their sugar did not meet the test requirements.

The Sugar Bounty was never popular with Vermont sugarmakers. Among reasons given were that "the weighing and sampling for the bounty would interfere with selling the first runs as soon as made," and, second, "that syrup would be worth more than sugar." But sugarmakers were urged by W.W.

Cooke, secretary of the board, and J.L. Hills, of the Agricultural Experiment Station, to take out the papers so "the farmer can make sugar or syrup as he pleases when the season opens, and still not lose the bounty if he finally decides to make sugar."

In both 1893 and 1894, 3,500 licenses were applied for. In the Thirteenth Vermont Agricultural Report by the State Board of Agriculture, Professor J.L. Hills (for whom the Hills Life Science Building at the University of Vermont is named) commented about several positive results of the Sugar Bounty, although most considered it to be a "flop":

> I thoroughly believe that the bounty system has been a great benefit to the Vermont sugar producer. It has given him an added incentive to good work; it has set a standard for him to strive to attain. The maple sugar does not seem to have fallen in price as cane sugar has done, so that the bounty is almost a gratuity. Its educational value in inducing the sugar maker to study methods has been great and two years experience has shown that weighing and sampling did not interfere with the selling of the product, and that the red-tape was in reality not a very great bugbear. In many cases the revenue stamp upon the package has aided in its sale, it being prima facie evidence of the purity of the goods. Whether the bounty system stands or falls, it has done a great and good work for the producers of the state, and its originators deserve their hearty thanks...Will the bounty law be in operation in 1894? We all know that the McKinley bill, like the earth, has been flattened at the polls, and that in all probability it will be repealed...I think it certain that the maple sugar bounty is doomed; but, on the other hand, I think it will last one year more. The applications have to be made by the first of July previous, and if the government accepts the application it becomes in a measure a party to a contract which it can hardly violate...The Maple Sugar Bounty has no friends among Washington officers. They claim that it has been ten times more bother and work to distribute $35,000 bounty among the 1,607 producers in Vermont, who succeeded in getting the bounty in 1892, than in distributing $7,000,000 among a few large planters of

Louisiana…They will undoubtedly use all their official power to prevent any such, to them, annoying work being again placed upon their department.

The *Fifteenth Agricultural Report by the State Board of Agriculture for the Year 1895* makes only a slight mention of the Sugar Bounty—a question to speaker Victor Spear: "What would you advise in regard to the collection of the bounty?" The answer was "To keep quiet and see what Congress proposes to do about it." It seems from this exchange that the bounty applications had been made, but payments had not been forthcoming. The lasting legacy of the Sugar Bounty, which had been unpopular with most independent Vermonters, consists of ornately decorated licenses, preserved in family records or framed on sugar house walls, treasured by the generations that came after.[78]

THE VERMONT MAPLE SUGARMAKERS' ASSOCIATION

It was in January 1893 that a group of men met in Morrisville to form the Vermont Maple Sugarmakers' Association. Their objectives were: "to improve quality, increase the quantity and protect manufacturers and consumers from the many fraudulent preparations placed on the market as pure maple goods." The association was among the first, if not *the* first, agricultural organization in the United States. Recognizing the potential of the organization, Professor Hills of the University of Vermont wrote in the *Thirteenth Vermont Agricultural Report for the Year 1893*:

> *The State in general, its soil, climate and men are well adapted to the growth of the trees and the making of the sugar. Vermont sugar and syrup have won a just reputation and enjoy the doubtful honor of giving a name to spurious goods [a backhanded way of saying the good name of Vermont maple products was being used to promote inferior products]. It is stated that there is more so-called Vermont sugar and syrup made in the city of Chicago, than in the entire State [of Vermont]. The sugarmakers of the State have wisely associated themselves for the purpose of*

bettering, enlarging and advertising the genuine product, and it is believed that the Vermont Maple Sugar Makers Association, founded at Morrisville, in January, 1893, will be a powerful factor in increasing the sale of the genuine Vermont maple sugar.[79]

In that same year, the Vermont Maple Sugarmakers' Association met its first major challenge in promoting Vermont maple products. The Vermont legislature was asked in 1890 to appropriate funds for a Vermont exhibit at the Chicago World's Fair of 1893. After careful consideration as to how the appropriation would benefit the state of Vermont, the proposal was funded and a commission was appointed. Since the legislature was predominantly made up of farmers, it was insisted that the largest portion of the exhibit feature Vermont agriculture, the major industry of the state. The initial appropriation was eventually doubled, then tripled in succeeding legislative sessions, due to the high price of construction. Nevertheless, the size of Vermont's building was dwarfed by Massachusetts and Maine, whose larger buildings were on either side of Vermont. The Vermont Maple Sugarmakers' Association was a significant component of the offerings of the Vermont building. An explanation of Vermont maple success at the Chicago World's Fair was written by H.H. McIntyre in the *1893–94 State Agriculture Board Report:*

An impression prevails among producers of high-grade Vermont maple sugar that consumers need education. They believe that the relative quantity of fabricated, spurious, adulterated, and low-grade goods put upon the market in this line is so great in comparison with the pure and good, that the majority of maple sugar users have set up a false standard of excellence by reason of total ignorance of the better article. It was with a view to correct this error that a special effort was made by the Commission and the Sugar Producers' Association to place an attractive and instructive exhibit of this product at the Exposition. A pavilion was built by the State in the gallery of the Department of Agriculture, at a cost of $1,500, filled with

Vermont Maple Sugarmakers' Association booklets preserve late-nineteenth-century history.

the finest sugar obtainable, and placed in charge of Mr. C. D. Whitman of Brattleboro...In addition to this, Mr. Whitman, knowing that however much the eye may be delighted with the soft-glowing colors of a fine syrup, the palate is, after all, the supreme judge and arbiter in the matter, obtained a "concession" and sold pancakes and syrup. If the Frenchman in the model bakery on the opposite side of the street thought the taste of Mr. Whitman's constant throng of customers, who turned their backs on French baking, crude and unappreciative of bons morceaux, he too needed education, and got it, perhaps before the season ended.[80]

From this report, it can be concluded that the first efforts of the Vermont Maple Sugarmakers' Association at education and advertisement were a "home run" for both the state and for its sugarmaking families. It was also an example of the long and strong cooperation between the sugarmakers and Vermont's agricultural officials that continues to this day.

Chapter 9

Vermont Maple Sugarmakers and the Pure Food and Drug Act

Q. In what way can the market be protected from the fraudulent sale of maple sugar?
A. I know of no way in which these foods can be kept out of our market, except by national legislation prohibiting their sale except as adulterated goods.
— *Victor I. Spear in the* Fifteenth Vermont Agricultural Report, 1895 *and* Sixteenth Vermont Agricultural Report, 1896

It is undoubtedly correct that the single greatest reason for the formation of the Vermont Maple Sugarmakers' Association was the effort to join forces to halt the widespread adulteration of maple products. In the *Fifteenth* and *Sixteenth Agricultural Report*, Victor I. Spear was an eloquent spokesperson for the sugarmakers. To gain a full appreciation for the plight of the maple industry, and how the industry supported the passage of a pure food act, Spear's address is presented in entirety:

> *Glucose Sugar. Although, as I have said, there is no possibility of overstocking the markets of the country with maple goods, there is a possibility that people will get more glucose than they want under the name of maple sugar. Not being supplied with maple trees with which to compete with Vermont in making*

maple sugar, the West, more especially Chicago and Omaha, have undertaken to supply the demand for maple sugar by putting on the market a combination of glucose and corn and maple sugar, and selling it as pure maple goods. Some of the poorest quality of Vermont maple sugar enters into the compound for flavoring purposes, and the darker the color and stronger the taste of the sugar used for this purpose, the higher the value.

Car loads of the last run of Vermont maple sugar orchards are sent to these cities each year for this purpose. I doubt if the Vermont sugar makers can afford to sell to this trade; it is better, I believe, to take in our buckets when the quality gets poor, than to make this inferior grade to put into the hands of enemies.

The adulterated maple goods trade is to the legitimate business, just what oleomargarine is to honest butter. They are both frauds, sold for what they are not, and owe their very existence to the lie that is placed upon them. I certainly believe that when Congress can let politics alone long enough to attend to the interests of the people a little, a pure food bill will be enacted that will compel the selling of all articles of food under their true name and with a guarantee of purity, with penalties for violation sufficient to prevent the offering of adulterated goods in the markets. The selling of adulterated maple sugar is entirely responsible for the low price now prevailing in the general markets of the country for maple products. So far as I know, every firm that is putting out these spurious goods has a Vermont brand, and in many instances put the name "Vermont" on to what they call their 2d or 3d class goods, thereby adding insult to injury.

Many of these firms use on their labels the name of some fictitious person as manufacturer, and give the residence as Vermont. In other cases they use the name of a town not in the state, and locate it in Vermont. The ingenious and various ways adopted to connect the name of Vermont with their goods, is the best possible recommend that the Vermont product could have, as people were never yet known to counterfeit an inferior article.

WHAT ARE WE TO DO ABOUT IT?[81]

Spear continued by stressing the importance of the passage of a "pure food law," but in the meantime praised the Vermont Maple Sugarmakers' Association, and urged "every farmer who makes a hundred pounds of maple sugar" to become a member. In the years 1894–95, membership had grown in just two to three years since the founding to six hundred sugarmakers. Spear described the development of an association label, to be used by members only, on "standard" maple goods, with the name and address of the maker. He also praised the association for holding meetings each winter, spurring excellence by awarding premiums for the best maple goods, and for publishing pamphlets detailing the best methods of preparing and marketing maple products. The Vermont Maple Sugarmakers' Association was flourishing!

PROGRESSING TOWARD A PURE FOOD AND DRUG ACT

Awareness of adulteration of Vermont maple syrup, and misleading labeling of products to associate the name "Vermont" with cheaper substances, mounted through the years. At the twelfth annual meeting of the Vermont Maple Sugarmakers' Association in Montpelier in January 1905, President Perry Chase, of East Fairfield, outlined the significant progress of the organization since its inception:

> *We have secured better laws against the adulteration of sugar and syrup, and attended to the enforcement of such laws when the facts have come to our knowledge that the laws have been broken. We have opened and extended the maple sugar trade with the cities and found markets for the Vermont sugar in the west. We have also found special customers for many producers who have manufactured a first class article of sugar or syrup and been obliged to place it on the general market; we have increased the confidence of our patrons from year to year and enlarged the trade; given the consumer a first class quality of genuine pure Vermont maple sugar and syrup; and above all have associated together a body of members who are ready, able and willing to do*

business at times, to protect the market, strengthen the confidence of the people, raise the standard of Vermont maple sugar and do all they can to make the production of the article a success and satisfy the consumer…So we must do all we can to make an article that will drive the false imitations out of the market. We must do as good old Governor Thomas Chittenden wrote to Washington that Vermonters would do if the New Yorkers did not let them alone. He said that Vermonters, in case of invasion, would retire to the vastnesses of their mountains and wage war on all creation. So we will do in the spring, as far as maple sugar goes, and we will sing the old song that they used to sing.

In this case, Perry Chase is not referring to New York and New Hampshire, but to invasion by the adulterators of Pure Vermont Maple Syrup, particularly those in the west—the sugarmakers "banners were unfurled":

Come New York and New Hampshire, come traitors and knaves,
If you rule o'er our sugar, ye rule o'er our graves;
Our vows are recorded, our banners unfurled,
With VERMONT MAPLE SUGAR, we defy all the world.

The next speaker on the program was A.R. Phillips, of Chagrin Falls, Ohio. Mr. Phillips shared the Ohio "Maple Sugar and Syrup Law," and urged Vermont sugarmakers to encourage a similar law for Vermont. He illustrated the need:

Let me call your attention to some of the uses of the word Maple as it is found upon labels of the adulterated article. Here are some of them:

"OPEN KETTLE MAPLE SYRUP."
How suggestive to the consumer that he is getting some of the real old pioneer maple syrup boiled down in the old cauldron kettle.
"LOG CABIN MAPLE SYRUP."
Don't that take the lover of maple sugar and syrup right back in

to the maple woods to the crude log cabin where our father boiled down the delicious stuff?
"MAPLE LEAF BRAND OF SUGAR AND SYRUP."
Beautiful isn't it.
"MAPLE SAP SYRUP" and, "SUGAR MAPLE SYRUP."
These are certainly a pair of sinners that need looking after.
"CRYSTAL ROCK MAPLE SYRUP."
Isn't that fine? Aren't they all beautiful? And don't they all say "Maple" in some form or other? And yet none of them say "The contents of this can (or package) contains Pure Maple Syrup, made wholly from the sap of the Maple tree"....Now here is another label that I saw in my own state just a few days before I came here, and I present it for your consideration, because I think you may be interested.
"PURE VERMONT SYRUP."
Here the word Maple is not used, but another word in its stead...to suggest to the innocent consumer that the package contains pure Maple syrup.[82]

At the conclusion of the 1905 meeting, the association passed several resolutions regarding maple laws, truth in labeling, adulteration and, most significantly, the following: "*Resolved.* That we again call the attention of our faithful members of the United States Senate and Congress to the deep interest which we feel in the passage of the so-called national pure food law."

VERMONT SENATOR REDFIELD PROCTOR AND TEDDY ROOSEVELT—THE PURE FOOD AND DRUG ACT OF 1906

The Vermont maple sugarmakers were smart guys and astute politicians! In the 1904 Vermont Maple Sugarmakers' Association booklet, which has a cover illustrating the newly proposed label to be used on the pure maple products of members, the list of members included all of the Vermont United States senators and representatives, including Senator Redfield Proctor. Also at the top of the list were the governor, and former governors, of the state. It is doubtful that all of these gentlemen were actually practicing sugarmakers. It is more likely that the Vermont Maple Sugarmakers' Association included the dignitaries in membership to secure their interest and maintain their awareness of issues concerning the Vermont maple industry.

Vermonter Redfield Proctor was a maple enthusiast and he had expressed interest in the safety protection of a pure food and drug bill, as well as the economic protection such a law would give by prevention of adulteration. But he became far more heavily involved with the promotion of a pure food bill due to a personal experience.

In a November 21, 1903 letter to Victor Spear, president of the Vermont Maple Sugarmakers' Association, Proctor wrote:

> *Dear Speare:*
>
> *Some of the leading grocers here are making a large display of bottles of "Towle's Log Cabin Maple Syrup." The label is that brand followed by "The Towle Maple Syrup Company, Burlington, Vt. St. Paul, Minn." We gave away what syrup we had last spring, and my butler got a bottle of this, but it is not maple syrup. I am going to see if they are amenable to the law for false branding, and would like to find out if they have any place of business in Burlington. I will enquire there, and perhaps you can. I cannot detect any maple taste in this, or very slight. If you have any leftover I wish you would send me the smallest box you put up of pint bottles, if you have any left, and I will not use this compound. I propose to visit the stores and show them the difference. One of them is a place where I have traded a good deal. If there is any way to bring the law to bear I will try it. My express franks are: American #623, Adams #068. Send bill.*
>
> *Very truly yours,*
> *Redfield Proctor*

Following this, Senator Proctor wrote to E. Burke, editor of the *Burlington Free Press*, inquiring whether there was, indeed, a company called "Towle Maple Syrup Co." in Burlington, Vermont. Burke published the letter in the *Free Press* without Proctor's knowledge. A

Vermont Maple Sugarmakers and the Pure Food and Drug Act

Mr. Beeman of Fairfax angrily responded that he had purchased $30,000 worth of maple sugar for the Towle Company the previous summer. In fact, the Towle Company was *not* located in Burlington. Vermont sugar, the poorest grade, was shipped west to the Towle Company in St. Paul, where it was blended, but the words "Burlington, Vermont" were on the label.

Although Proctor was certain that what he had tasted was not maple syrup, he found the adulteration could not be proved. He wrote to Mr. Beeman that adulteration by beet or cane sugar could not be chemically detected, but he would like to see an oath by the Towle Company that they were not using beet or cane sugar in their Vermont-labeled product. His final comment in a letter to A.F. Palmer Jr. of Waterbury was: "I think it is largely of cane sugar, and of course that gives room for a very large profit."

The January 7, 1904 issue of the *Burlington Free Press* reported on the annual meeting of the Vermont Sugarmakers' Association. Within the report was a mention of a speech by Secretary A.J. Croft: "He also spoke in complimentary terms of the Vermont delegation for the work they were doing for the farmers of the State and mentioned the visit of Senator Proctor to the meeting on Tuesday night, in particular, thanking him for his interest in the passage of the pure food bill."

Finally, in a November 15, 1905 letter to Theodore Roosevelt, Senator Proctor wrote:

> *Dear Mr. President:*
>
> *I have not bothered you with suggestions about your message, but I hope you will say a word in favor of Pure Food legislation. I think that would insure prompt action, for I don't think there is serious, direct opposition. It is more to embarrass and delay and this is stimulated by parties who have pecuniary interests that they fear would suffer. But that every man, woman and child in the country may eat and drink what is free as possible from harmful adulteration is, it seems to me, of vital importance to the welfare of the country. On account of high prices the temptations for adulterations are great.*
>
> *Very respectfully, yours,*
> *Redfield Proctor*[83]

The first Pure Food and Drug Act passed the Senate on June 30, 1906, and became effective on January 1, 1907. Redfield Proctor died on March 4, 1908. He and the Vermont Maple Sugarmakers' Association had contributed to the enactment of a law (improved in 1938) that to this day permits pursuit of adulteration violations. To protect the consumer of Pure Vermont Maple Syrup, the laws are vigorously enforced. When a container is purchased with those words prominently displayed, one can be confident that the syrup is backed by the strength of the Pure Food and Drug Act, the Vermont Agency of Agriculture, the Vermont Sugarmakers' Association and the laws of the Vermont legislature!

Chapter 10

Big Business

The Making of a Maple Magnate
—George C. Cary—and Afterwards

Until the dawn of the new century, maple sugar and maple syrup were largely consumed by families, shared with relatives and friends and sold or traded locally. The first large Vermont packing company began accidentally, in "mud season."[84] An article that appeared in the January 1929 issue of the *Vermonter* magazine—"America's Maple Sugar King: George C. Cary"—told about a salesman who came to build a large maple factory in St. Johnsbury and "wheel and deal" in a maple sugar business. The story began in the late 1800s. A native of Maine, he sold wholesale groceries in Vermont for a Maine firm:

> *I used to travel all over the northern part of the state, stopping in Morrisville and Craftsbury and Newport. You know what these country roads are like in the spring? Well, one particular spring they seemed worse than usual, and when I arrived in North Craftsbury on my regular trip it was impossible to get any further, the roads were so soft and slumpy.*
>
> *I stayed at the village during the afternoon of that day planning to start early the following morning when the roads would be frozen—which I did do. On the side I tried to do a little business, but I was not successful.*
>
> *Finally, one man said that he would give me an order for groceries if I would take my pay in maple sugar. He said he had*

The Cary Maple Sugar Plant, early 1900s. *Courtesy of the New England Maple Museum.*

fifteen hundred pounds, and would sell it at four and a half cents [per pound]. *I saw that this was probably the only chance I had of getting an order so I told him we'd call it a trade, and I sold him the groceries.*

I went back to Portland and informed my firm what I had done, and they told me that if I had bought the sugar I would have to get rid of it.

That very week I came in contact with a tobacco man from Richmond, Virginia, who was trying to push his product. At that time they were introducing cut-plug tobacco, and out of curiosity I asked him how it was made. He explained that the leaves were dipped in West Indies sugar for the dual purposes of flavoring and causing them to stick together when pressed.

I found that he was paying five cents a pound for this sugar, and it occurred to me that here might be an opportunity to dispose of my maple sugar, so I asked him why this could not be used instead of the West Indies sugar. Of course, this was something which had never been tried, or even thought of. We discussed the possibilities of the idea for some time, but he did not dare to buy much of this maple sugar, even when I offered it for a half a cent less than he was paying for the other.

Finally, I told him that if he would buy my fifteen hundred pounds I would agree to sell one hundred boxes of his plug tobacco on my next Vermont trip; but he was a cautious soul and would take only two hundred pounds of my sugar. He experimented with this amount, however, and at the end of my third Vermont trip I received a letter from him ordering a thousand pounds of sugar.[85]

From that fifteen hundred pounds of sugar, taken in payment for a grocery order, emerged an industry which grew to not only supply tobacco manufacturers but also candy makers and producers of blended syrups. Maple sugar was obtained from Vermont, but also from Canada, depending on crop circumstances and various political situations.

A large, four-story brick building was constructed in St. Johnsbury, which is now the home of the Maple Grove Company. In the early to mid-1900s, carloads of sugar and candy were shipped all over the United States, and some went as far as Cuba, the Philippines,

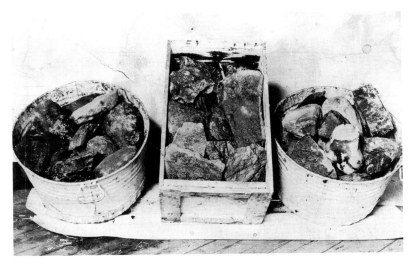

Sugar chunks at Cary Maple Sugar Company. *Courtesy of the New England Maple Museum.*

Packaging maple sugar at the Cary plant. *Courtesy of the New England Maple Museum.*

the Hawaiian Islands, London and Alaska. Another factory also existed in Lennoxville, Quebec.

Not satisfied with merely buying other farmers' maple sugar, George Cary purchased a four-thousand-acre farm in North Danville, Vermont, which he named Highland Farm. There he raised cattle and produced "the finest maple sugar that can be made" from twenty thousand maple trees. On his farm, George Cary set up a demonstration of the evolution of maple sugaring, devoting one section to the Native People's trough and wooden spout method; one to metal spouts and buckets, hauling sap with oxen and a bobsled; and one in which he experimented with an elaborate and extensive (but impractical) *metal* pipeline system. Using Highland Farm and the Cary Maple Sugar Company, a motion picture company made a 35mm silent movie in 1927 about the harvest, manufacture and marketing of Vermont maple syrup and candy.[86]

A division of Cary Maple Sugar Company known as Maple Grove Candies, Inc. was first incorporated January 1920 by George,

Cary and Highland maple syrup labels, designed for promotion. *Courtesy of the New England Maple Museum.*

three women from New York and three from St. Johnsbury. In 1929, George Cary and a partner bought out the other stockholders and formed Maple Grove Candies, Inc. A brick building was constructed in front of the Cary factory.

In 1931, the Cary Company business faltered, then failed; it was rumored that an order for several million pounds of maple sugar from the American Tobacco Co. had fallen through, although the sugar had been bought and placed in inventory. Lacking funds to pay the company's debts, listing liability to creditors of $3,221,046 and assets of $102,004, George Cary filed for bankruptcy in September of 1931. On November 21 of that year, he died.[87]

THE EARLY VERMONT MAPLE PACKERS, THE VERMONT MAPLE SUGARMAKERS' MARKET AND MORE

George Cary had established the fact that there was a large market for Vermont maple syrup, and that did not escape the notice of other entrepreneurs. The American Maple Company in Newport began to buy and sell, as did United Maple in Essex Junction. It is little known that in 1904, and possibly earlier, the Vermont Maple

Early-twentieth-century syrup bottle, Vermont Maple Sugarmaker's Market label.

Sugarmakers' Association also endeavored to market maple syrup, under an organization called The Vermont Maple Sugar Makers' Market. The entire back of the 1904 Vermont Maple Sugarmakers' Association booklet was devoted to the following advertisement:

> *The Vermont Maple Sugar Makers' Market*
> *Have a steadily increasing trade for Pure High Grade Maple Syrup and Sugar…The members of the Vermont Maple Sugar Makers' Association will find a profitable outlet for all their products through this market…Victor I Spear, Manager, and Homer W. Vail, Treasurer, of the The Vermont Maple Sugar Makers' Association, will give their personal attention to the grading and marketing of all consignments. Give the market a trial shipment of your best goods and watch results…* JACKETED CANS OR BARRELS FOR SHIPPING SYRUP FURNISHED ON APPLICATION. *Liberal cash advances on consignments when desired. Vermont Maple Sugar Makers' Market, Randolph, VT.*

The Market also advertised in the 1905 and 1909 booklets. At the same time, the Vermont Maple Sugarmakers' Association was displaying an official label to be used by members for their "Pure Maple Products of good quality…100 of which are furnished free of charge, if requested, with name and address printed on them, to each member on receipt of $1.00 for membership fee. Additional labels at 50 cents per 100."

Marketing became a mix of individual efforts of the farmer, including roadside stands and signs directing buyers to the farmhouse, and packers who would take on the work of larger marketing efforts. Packers were also supplying companies such as the Towle Log Cabin Company, for their blended maple and cane syrup.

Chapter 11

How Do the Maple Trees Tick?
Solvers of the Mysteries!

Vermont has a strong history in maple research. It started at the University of Vermont in the 1880s and it is still today the most important center of maple research in the world…first and foremost any new advances must be tested to make sure they leave us with the same great flavor that we expect from pure Vermont maple syrup.

— *David Marvin, in the video*
Pure Vermont Maple: A Proud Tradition

Appreciation for the tradition of maple research in Vermont is essential to comprehending the world-wide role that the University of Vermont has played in understanding the maple tree and maintaining the quality of pure maple syrup. It is one element that has helped to make Pure Vermont Maple the renowned product it is!

PROFESSORS W.W. COOKE AND J.L. HILLS

Research into the mystery of the maple tree that produces the slightly sweet sap that is the basis for Vermont's maple sugar and syrup began in 1891 with the work of Professors W.W. Cooke and J.L. Hills. They published *State Agricultural Experiment Station Bulletin No. 26—Maple Sugar*. The slim volume described to Vermont sugarmakers and others the steps necessary to make sugar qualifying for the bounty. Provisions of the bounty were also included in the booklet, along with a description of the polariscope, an instrument that determined the amount of sugar in a sample. The booklet was intended to guide the sugarmaker toward success in achieving bounty payments. For a time, Professor Cooke was charged by the U.S. government with evaluation of the sugar presented by bounty applicants.[88]

Maple researchers seem driven by a curiosity that leads them to delve into the science of the maple tree, a determination to solve problems that might affect the production of the best possible Vermont maple syrup and a desire to share the information with sugarmakers in the Green Mountain State and elsewhere. Hills and Cooke were followed by a long line of maple researchers that continues today.

Research in the Mountains—"C.H." Jones and Colleagues

The first to follow Cooke and Hills was C.H. Jones, a colorful chemistry professor noted for his humor and his penchant for poetry whom Hills recruited in 1896. Mary Lighthall, a young chemistry student at the university, revered "C.H.," describing his personality and work in an unpublished paper.[89]

According to Mary Lighthall, C.H. convinced Dean Hills that the university needed to have a live sugarbush for maple study. They leased Melandy Hill sugar place, in Jeffersonville, about twenty miles from Burlington, and stayed in a hotel run by the Melandys, traveling to Jeffersonville by train. In spite of very poor laboratory conditions (a hotel room for headquarters), a 164-page "masterpiece of understanding of tree physiology" was produced, *The Maple Sap Flow*.

A later important study, which took more than two years, involving analyzing tree sections in all seasons, *The Carbohydrate Contents of the Maple Tree*, also added significantly to scientific understanding of *Acer saccharum*. However, in the eyes of sugarmakers, C.H. Jones will always be most revered throughout the maple world for his famous

How Do the Maple Trees Tick? Solvers of the Mysteries!

Early sap flow experiments at the Proctor Farm. *Courtesy of the Proctor Maple Research Center.*

calculation that allows anyone to determine quickly the amount of syrup that will be made from sap when the sugar content of the sap has been measured. An average amount of sugar in maple sap is about 2 or 2.5 percent, but there are a few trees that consistently yield 8 to 10 percent sugar, requiring far less boiling to make syrup. And trees in a deeply wooded forest are likely to have sap which is merely 1 percent. Why? The phenomenon of the 10 percent tree has not been definitively explained; it is likely genetic, comparable to athletes who have the superior ability to achieve above and beyond the competition. The poorly producing 1 percent tree in the forest is more easily understood—forest trees are competing for the moisture, nutrients and sunlight required for sugar production. Long after sharing the formula and sugarmaking hints with farmers, C.H. immortalized his work in a poem in Burlington, Vermont, in December 1946:

> *"Maple Rule of 86"*
>
> *For many years, throughout its life*
> *The maple tree so dear*
> *Has stored, with other woody growth*
> *A liquid sweet and clear.*

Maple Sugarin' in Vermont

When winter cold is followed by
Warm days with frost at night,
When spring is surely on the way
We know the time is right.

Again we look ahead with joy
To Vermont's yearly treat,
When maple trees are tapped to get
Our share of Nature's sweet.

Get all equipment ready, for
The season soon is here,
Be ready for the early runs,
The best ones of the year.

Put all your maple trees to work
The sugar's waiting there.
Then, when the too brief season ends
You'll surely have your share.

If quality you strive to get
Long with much syrup too,
Then all utensils must be clean—
You'll find this always true.

Don't let the sap stand long in pails
Or tanks of any kind.
The sooner that each run is boiled
The better grade you'll find.

Perchance the fancy grade is missed.
I'm sure we all agree
These days a ready sale is found
For grades one, two and three.

With prices also at top notch
You cannot fail to score,

How Do the Maple Trees Tick? Solvers of the Mysteries!

Remember, though, the season lasts
At best—one month—no more.

It's quite the fashion now to know
A fact on which to bank—
The sugar content of the sap
From trees and storage tank.

A sap hydrometer is used
Which quickly tells this tale.
It shows that trees will vary much
In sweetness in each pail.

The average figure known, you find
The syrup that it makes:
How many gallons of your sap
Each syrup gallon takes.

You ask me how the problem's solved?
It's easy, all you do,
Divide the Number Eighty-Six*
By sugar content true.

Thus two percent takes forty-three
And five but seventeen;
The average, say three percent,
Takes twenty-nine, 'tis seen.

The richer sap, without a doubt,
Will save you many a dime
In quality and fuel cost
And also boiling time.

Another maple season, boys,
Looms just around the bend,
It may be good, it may be poor;
One can't predict the trend.

For weather, you all know, still holds
A variable hand.
That's just another reason why
Our cards some tricks should land.

So get equipment ready <u>now</u>
For what may be your lot.
<u>Make sure, corral all early runs</u>—
Be Johnny-on-the-spot.

*To use this rule in Canada
It slightly changed must be
For there the number eighty-six
Becomes one hundred three.

NEW GUYS ON THE MAPLE RESEARCH BLOCK—DRS. MARVIN AND TAYLOR AND THE PROCTOR FARM

In 1943, Dr. James Marvin and Dr. Fred Taylor began their maple research at the University of Vermont. Mary Lighthall describes Jim Marvin as "full of energy—always running, not walking. It was hard to keep up with him going across campus!" I can describe Fred Taylor as a quiet, gentle, unassuming person—ready to help, declining to use the title "Dr. Taylor." Fred's shared bits of information have contributed immeasurably to this book.

For three years, Marvin and Taylor rented sugarbushes in the Underhill area with the assistance of Arthur Packard Sr., president of the Vermont Farm Bureau. "What we came up with eventually was the fact that not all sugarbushes are alike. A lot of farmers have to boil off a lot more water than others do simply because they have trees that don't produce quite as much sugar as their neighbors do." Knowing some of the experiments necessary would require "radical surgery" that they could not ask sugarmakers to allow them to perform on their trees, Marvin and Taylor convinced Governor Mortimer Proctor, of the Proctor marble family (another Proctor to the rescue of the maple industry!) to purchase and donate to the university the Harvey Farm in Underhill Center. Consisting of approximately two hundred acres, the land abounded in sugar maples. Acquired in 1946, the Proctor Farm (later renamed the Proctor Maple Research Center) became a center of maple research known throughout the world.

The first lab, a diminutive building, one hundred square feet in size, is now a national historic landmark. In a 1988 interview, Fred Taylor described it: "We used to call it 'the shanty'—which was smaller than the average bathroom, but we crowded all our instruments into it; we crowded all the people into it at lunchtime, and it served a good purpose…it was constructed in Burlington… The building was on runners, and it was put on a flatbed trailer and hauled up into the woods, where it still stands."

The first Proctor Farm research lab, listed on the National Register of Historic Places.

Fred Taylor, a founder and researcher at the Proctor Farm. *Courtesy of the Proctor Maple Research Center.*

Some instruments needed for their research were not available—they had to be invented by someone who liked to "tinker." Fred explained:

> *Jim was a great one for adapting existing instrumentation and tools and so on, for different purposes...these recording devices were products of his—I was going to say—imagination—but not exactly that, but his vision. [Like Mary Lighthall, Fred describes Jim Marvin's energy]...followin' that guy around through knee-deep snow really made a man outa me! Or made me old before my time, I've forgotten which![90]*

Eventually a sugarhouse and a proper laboratory were built at the Proctor Farm, and research assistant Mary Lighthall was hired with funding assistance from General Foods. Then began a long line of researchers—Marvin and Taylor were joined by Fred Laing, Italian scientist Dr. Mariafranca Morselli, Sumner Williams and many more—all working to solve some of the maple mysteries. But it was Marvin and Taylor who have the distinction of fathering the Proctor Farm, with the financial help of Mortimer Proctor.

Today the Proctor Maple Research Center facilities include an up-to-date, well-equipped laboratory and two modern research sugarhouses.

Chapter 12

Teaching and Learning—for Sugarmakers *and* Consumers

Men, women, maple sugar and horses
The first are strong, the latter fleet,
The second and third are exceedingly sweet,
And all are uncommonly hard to beat.
—From Bulletin 38, 1929, published by E.H. Jones, commissioner
of agriculture and the Vermont Bureau of Publicity, Montpelier

Vermonters sometimes say they've been "sugarin' from the time they could walk—there's always something you can do!" Sugarmaking knowledge has been passed on from father and mother to son and daughter, in many instances for more than seven generations, since the time of the settlers. Knowledge is always shared with neighbors when new arrivals need to get started in sugaring. First and foremost, it's the sharing that perpetuates Vermont's maple industry.

Beginning in 1872, biennial reports were written by the Vermont Board of Agriculture, Manufacturing and Mining, and later by the commissioner of agriculture. The reports detailed *every* aspect of Vermont's agriculture. They are replete with fascinating historical data—as well as statistics, laws, inspection data, marketing information and much more—to inform the farmer. The maple industry was always an element of the report, and in later years the books contained the annual Vermont Sugarmakers' Association meeting report.

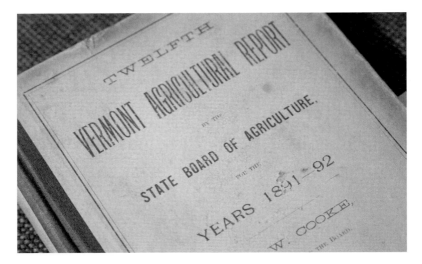

Vermont Agricultural Report 1891–92.

"How does the *syrup* flow out of the tree during the *summer?*" Of course it's the sap that flows from the tree, not syrup, and that happens only in late winter and spring. It was likely similar questions, which heightened the awareness that consumers needed to be educated, that prompted the Department of Agriculture to produce Bulletin 21 and, later, Bulletin 38. According to Agriculture Commissioner E.H. Jones, the booklet was "designed to furnish information to consumers, school students and others who are interested in maple products rather than a manual for sugar makers." The poem found at the beginning of this chapter is taken from Bulletin 38, which also contained detailed information about maple products, production, history and recipes. The booklet was reprinted year after year and widely distributed. It now takes the form of a pamphlet, *The Story of Maple Time in Vermont*, published by the Vermont Maple Sugarmakers' Association.

As the industry became more organized, meetings, journals, gazetteers, books and bulletins also became sources of information. The Vermont Maple Sugarmakers' Association held annual January meetings, beginning in 1894. Speakers were chosen who presented information, and new equipment was demonstrated and advertised.

Sap Spout advertisements, found in a Vermont Maple Sugarmakers' Association booklet.

For several years, the association published booklets with the text of speeches, questions, information and advertisements; members who had not attended were able to be fully educated about the issues and learn about the latest innovations. Those who did attend had an opportunity to get together in the slower time of mid-winter and socialize, just prior to the beginning of the new season.

In 1934, the Vermont Union Agricultural Council was formed, and also began to hold annual meetings in January. The maple industry was a member of the council, and the Vermont Maple Sugarmakers' meeting then coincided, and was later combined, with the four-day council meeting. In the *1939–1940 Report of the Commissioner of Agriculture*, E.H. Jones wrote: "The Vermont Union Agricultural Council which is composed of all the principal agricultural organizations of the state and is sponsored by the Department of Agriculture and the Extension Service, continues to provide an excellent medium for the coordination of the interest of

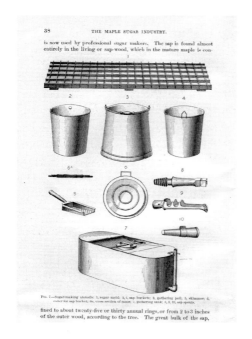

38   THE MAPLE SUGAR INDUSTRY.

Recommended sugaring equipment, 1905 USDA publication.

the member units…It is the outstanding agricultural event of the year." The Vermont Agricultural Council event evolved into the existing Vermont Farm Show. In a video interview, Everett Willard told of "the farm boys" looking forward to this event, then held in Burlington's Memorial Auditorium.[91]

The University of Vermont Extension Service was the agency charged with carrying the information and recommendations of the University of Vermont Experiment Station and the U.S. and Vermont Departments of Agriculture to farm families. In a video interview, Ray Foulds, who became an Extension Service forester in 1948, told about his feelings of responsibility toward sugarmakers, and his desire to help them: "Several of them began to say to me, 'Gee, if I didn't make this syrup and sell it, I couldn't stay on the farm, because I have to pay the grain bill and I have to pay taxes with the sugar and syrup I boil in the spring.'" To help the farmers, Ray Foulds instituted January maple schools in 1949. Meetings with noon dinners were held in each county, where speakers from various agencies disseminated the latest information and equipment dealers displayed their wares. Ray was also instrumental in launching the E.H. Jones Maple Industry Improvement Contest, which lasted for several years, spurring competition and overall interest in quality. He explained: "It selected the top sugarmaker in each county and finally, the state winner…and the organizations involved in that contest were Forests and Parks, the Department of Agriculture, Extension Service, Farm Bureau, and the College of Agriculture. The judges went around and judged each county winner, then picked the State winner."[92] The state winner in 1949 was Noah Fleury; his prize was a handsome gold watch, engraved around the edge with the words "Vermont Maple Sugarmakers"—a recognition made by the Sugarmakers' Association to one of their own.

Lucien Paquette tells of his work as Addison County Extension Agent. Feeling a kinship with his county sugarmakers, and determined to expand sugaring, Lucien used a summer intern to survey the county, identifying where expansion might occur. Upon his retirement, the active Addison County Maple Sugarmakers' Association made Lucien a lifetime member in appreciation for his efforts.[93]

Chapter 13

Stories From the Heart of Maple Country

"WEATHER HOLDS A VARIABLE HAND"

Maple helped feed sugarmaking families in an early disastrous weather instance. The year 1816 was a particularly devastating one, known as "The Year without a Summer" or "1816 and Froze to Death." There was frost in every month of the year, and plants were killed just as they began to grow. Walter Crockett wrote that "fish was a common article of diet. It is related that fish were never so plentiful in the Missisquoi River as during the famine period. People from the eastern part of the State came in large numbers to barter maple sugar and other articles for fish."[94]

Walter Crockett also described another strange weather occurrence: "The winter of 1847–1848 was unseasonably mild. Violets were picked on New Year's Day, peepers were heard in January, and a live butterfly was sighted on February 4." Without a sufficient opportunity for the hard freeze of winter, it was unlikely that there could have been much of a maple crop in the spring of 1848.[95]

Fierce weather had an even more serious effect on the maple industry. The winds of the 1938 hurricane dealt a heavy blow. A survey of damage to the state listed the destruction of 1,354,000 sugar maple trees and the loss of, or damage to, 1,756 sugar houses.

The commissioner of agriculture wrote: "Maple sugar orchards were especially vulnerable to the wind and as new trees are not utilized for tapping until they reach the age of approximately 40 years, the loss of such a great number is greatly regretted."[96]

BILL CLARK BUILDS A SUGARHOUSE

The line from the "Rule of 86" poem "For weather you all know still holds a variable hand" was as telling an adage then as it is today. Without the necessary fluctuations in temperature, maple production is limited. The year before C.H. wrote his poem, 1945, had been one of the *worst* sugaring seasons in history.

Wilson "Bill" Clark had a brand-new sugarhouse that year. Bill, age fourteen, who would eventually be president of the Vermont Maple Sugarmakers' Association for more than thirty years, had begun sugaring with his brother Jack two years earlier in 1943, when Bill was twelve and Jack was ten. They sugared in a lean-to, and used equipment from around the dairy farm: "the front bob of a one horse sled with 6 milk cans to collect" and "Grandpa Streeter boiling on an old open stone boiling place."

In 1945, Bill wrote in his scrapbook: "The sugar season of 1945 was a short one." An Associated Press clipping in Bill's scrapbook, taken from the *Rutland Herald*, acknowledged that "the maple season in VERMONT was a bare two weeks." There was an abnormally early run before most sugarmakers had tapped; it caught many by surprise. Then an unseasonably warm bout of temperatures followed that caused the trees to bud early.

This was disappointing to Bill and Jack, a couple of schoolboys who eventually used the label "The Clark Brothers" on their products. During the previous summer, they had cut trees and dragged enough logs from the woods to dress nearly 1,800 board feet of lumber, with which they had built a bona-fide sugarhouse. But by 1946, the boys were well equipped. Their dad had bought a used Leader evaporator, a new three-barrel gathering tank and a fifteen-barrel storage tank. They were eager to meet the 1946 season, which was only somewhat more favorable. Bill and Jack made seventy gallons of syrup, some of which they sold at the wartime OPA (Office of Price Administration) ceiling price of $3.39 a gallon. At the end of the season, they had advance orders for their 1947 crop.[97]

Records of the Cary Maple Sugar company confirm the woes of the 1945 season, but they also tell of a short crop in 1946. The company was able to purchase only about 65 percent of their normal needs. In 1947, when the wartime ceiling was removed, the price of Vermont maple syrup jumped from the OPA price of $3.39 a gallon to $7.00 a gallon for fancy syrup. The Cary records tell a twentieth-century maple story. They contain summaries of each year from 1902 to 1967, when the company was absorbed by the Fred Fear Baltimore food company (which, not long after, sold the buildings and disbanded operations). Crop records, syrup prices and weather records are included in the details.

Weather is not the only problem faced by sugarmakers. Over the years, tent caterpillars, other insects and diseases have plagued the trees and affected the maple crop. On threatening occasions, the Department of Agriculture, scientists from the University of Vermont, the Experiment Station and the Extension Service have worked together to provide sugarmakers with the research and information necessary to deal as effectively as possible with the problems.

MAPLE SUGAR SWEETENS LIFE

The lives of the Native Peoples and the settlers were enriched by the gift of the sugar maple tree, and maple sugar continued to lighten the spirits of Vermonters who came after.

Fred Taylor wrote a World War I anecdote for the 1993 *Vermont Maplerama Booklet*: "During World War I, in response to an appeal from the YMCA, 500 pounds of maple sugar were sent to American troops in France." As terrible an experience as the war was, those who received the maple sugar knew that Vermonters at home were thinking of them.

The Depression of 1929 caused Vermonters to rely on maple sugar from their own farms. Evelyn Stanley wrote that "During the Great Depression of the 1930's maple sugar...was a blessing for the homemaker…even more so into the World War II era…the sugar stamps were not nearly enough to supply her with white sugar for the sweets demanded by a tableful of hired help."[98]

During World War II, a five-pound box of maple sugar was dropped from a helicopter to a G.I. in the Philippines—likely received by a Vermont boy missing his taste of home.

Marjorie Palmer Learns to Sugar

Sitting in a rocking chair in her Shelburne sugarhouse, Marjorie Palmer chuckled as she related her World War II story during a video interview:

You want to know how I got started in sugaring? Well, it was many years ago during the war when there was a shortage of sugar and I had small children at the time. And the sugar coupons never seemed to stretch enough. So we had this sugar place at the farm—we lived in the city at the time—and I had been up there and seen the buckets and the old evaporator so I said to my husband, "I think I'll sugar," and he said, "Do you know how?" and I said, "No, but I can read." And at the time we had a man working for us and his wife was going to college, University of Vermont. And so I went down and asked her if she'd like to sugar and she said, "Why I don't know anything about it, do you?" I said, "No, but we can read." And so the two of us being young and ignoramuses at the time we waltzed up to the "top of the line," to Jim Marvin, who was the head of the Proctor Research, and asked him all about it. He was wonderful to us, and told us all he could. And another man who was head of Leader Evaporator was very nice to us and told us things we'd need to get started. We had one old white horse, slower than molasses, and I bought a little rig that would hold 4 milk cans, and we used those. There was an old barn that had fallen down, and her husband lugged all the wood up to the sugar place, and one would boil, and the other would gather then the other one would boil and the other one would gather. Of course it was up

Children helped—a small gathering rig in the Coombs collection.

and down, splashing. We had a wonderful time! And I'm telling you we thought that syrup was wonderful. 'Course it was awful black, but we thought it was great anyhow! And that was the beginning, and once you've begun it's like taking dope—you're hooked. And you never get over it—it runs in your blood.

MARY COOMBS MAKES CANDY

Mary Coombs and her husband Robert founded Coombs Maple Candy, beginning in their kitchen, graduating to the basement of the Weldon Hotel in Greenfield, Massachusetts, and finally building and then enlarging a factory in Jacksonville. Here, for many years, they made and shipped their famous candy. Their son, Bob, accumulated a large collection of maple antiques in his travels buying and selling maple for the company. His items, now in the possession of a family member, have helped to preserve the history of the Vermont maple industry.

We always gathered with horses. They used the round sap sled, one stave stuck up, so you could hang on. The sap sled they used was a straight sled and in the woods there was lots of "dip holes", the sled would go into a dip hole and then when they went up the other side the sap would slop all over, you'd get it all down your front. Before the horses, my father used oxen. He had a pair of white oxen, and they seemed to know just where to stop. They'd gather all the buckets around this area and then they'd say "get-up," to the oxen, and they'd go along to the next group and they'd stop. They travelled slower than the horses, but they were very trustworthy.

TRUMAN YOUNG CHEWS GUM

As I look back I've got an interesting story that happened. I wasn't 8–9 years old I guess, and back then the sap pails leaked quite often. And the man that owned the woods where my father worked used to have me walk around the woods to find the ones that were leaking, and the way I would stop the leak is he would come up here in the morning, and he had a long overcoat I remember, and he had deep pockets in it, and he had those pockets full of chewin' gum, and he'd walk with me over to the bush and he'd want me to start chewin' gum, so I'd chew gum, and I'd walk 'round and if I saw a leak I'd stick the gum in to fill the hole, and he was right there watching me. I'd go all around the whole woods. And at night I'd come home and I was sick, I couldn't eat. My mother used to holler at him about me chewin' so much gum, of course it upset my stomach. And the next day he'd be right up there with chewin' gum again, and I'd go around chewin' gum and sticking it in, filling the holes, and that was my earliest experience in the bush.

Although this cannot be considered an approved sanitary practice, any germs little Truman had would have boiled away with the heat of the evaporator! Truman became a renowned sugarmaker, frequently winning prizes at the Vermont Farm Show and at the Vermont State Fair in Rutland.

HELEN NEARING WRITES *THE MAPLE SUGAR BOOK*

Helen Nearing, with her husband, Scott, wrote *The Maple Sugar Book*, a scholarly exploration of the maple syrup industry in the United States and Canada. I was asked by the Vermont Maple History

The author interviews Helen Nearing.

Committee to visit Helen at her home in Harborside, Maine, and interview her about the history of writing her book:

> *Scott was writing a book about war. So I went to the Rare Book Rooms in the New York Public Library and looked, from scratch, for anything on sugaring. I went through Dutch, German, Swedish, English and French books and looked in the indices and flipped through the books—all these wonderful old, ancient books, and there I found my material. After days of this I showed it to Scott and he said "You've got stuff for a book there...And in many of the books I read, it was not known whether the French taught the Indians or the Indians taught the French how to make maple sugar. And from the historic records I could find that the Indians taught the French.*

The Nearings had settled in southern Vermont and operated an extensive sugarbush set up with metal pipeline. Too close to the Stratton Mountain ski area, they left for the coast of Maine because the area had become "non-Vermontish." Helen's extensive knowledge of languages, her research and her sugaring background combined to produce a sugarmaking classic.

147

Chapter 14

The Move to Gain More Money from the Maple Crop

When the hard work of making maple syrup was finished, and the season came to a close, selling the crop was the next step. Some was given or sold to neighbors. Some was put up to sell to the occasional farm visitor. What to do with the remainder? Most was sold in bulk to plants such as the Cary Company for a price established by the company. Harold Howrigan of Fairfield tells the story of his brother Francis's job as a young man, working for the Cary Company at the Fairfield Railroad Station. Pulled by horses, wagons filled with fifty-five-gallon drums of maple syrup arrived at the station.

Francis's job was to unload the barrels, weigh them on the platform scale, then load them onto a train bound for Newport, from where they were conveyed to the Cary plant in St. Johnsbury. For this, Francis received two dollars a day. Maple syrup weighs eleven pounds per gallon—Francis was handling barrels weighing more than six hundred pounds! (Eventually, he became a prominent figure in the Vermont Senate, and was the person who successfully sponsored the bill that made Pure Vermont Maple Syrup the "Official Flavor of Vermont," along with Hazel Prindle of Charlotte, who shepherded the bill through the House of Representatives.)

One group of sugarmakers banded together to bypass the packers by forming a cooperative to promote and market the

Maple sugar with Vermont labels was shipped in cans. The lids are embossed with "Vermont Maple Sugar."

product. Located in Essex, it was begun by Arthur Packard and his associates. A broadside featuring a photo of Arthur Packard tells the story of the Vermont Maple Cooperative:

We GAINED new markets without SELLING EXPENSE.

Arthur H. Packard, President of the Vermont Maple Cooperative, Inc. tells how the cooperative, working with chain stores, increased the sale of maple syrup and developed new markets in sections where maple syrup had never been sold before.

By Arthur H. Packard.

Back in 1932 it looked as if the maple syrup producers of Vermont would have no outlet for their new crop. There was such a large carry-over from the three previous years, that we were advised not to tap our trees at all...Producers were selling in bulk and at retail wherever they could, but as individuals they had no way of increasing the sale of their syrup...The Directors of our Cooperative decided to pack our members' highest quality syrup in half pint bottles under our own brand, and try to interest the chain stores in merchandising the product...When we approached the chain stores with our proposition, they

The Move to Gain More Money from the Maple Crop

responded by taking the entire 1932 output of our new brand of maple syrup—the "Co-op Brand." They have been our largest customers ever since, buying about ninety percent of our bottled syrup at a price that gives a fair return to our members…Today we are shipping maple syrup into territories where people never bought maple syrup before.

Arthur Packard encouraged others throughout Vermont to form cooperatives. One, the Groton Maple Sap Cooperative, Inc., evidently failed. A record book found in a Groton barn contained letters from Packard, a stock certificate and bank evidence of a financial difficulty. The Vermont Maple Cooperative facility eventually became the home of a packing company, United Maple, when the Vermont Maple Cooperative ceased operations.

One cooperative has been highly successful and long lasting. According to Harold Howrigan of Fairfield and Bruce Martell of the Vermont Agency of Agriculture, the Franklin County Cooperative has been good for Vermont maple farmers, establishing an organization that can obtain fair prices, and a place where bulk buyers can go with assurance that they are purchasing syrup tested and graded by the Vermont Agency of Agriculture.

Not everyone was satisfied with the prices set for bulk syrup, particularly those determined by the Cary Company. A man from Virginia, retired to a farm in Arlington, initiated attempts to change the status quo—Colonel Fairfax Ayres purchased two additional nearby farms, eventually owning 3,500 buckets and producing some seven hundred to one thousand gallons of syrup annually. He developed a strong interest in pricing! *Time* magazine, in a March 31, 1947 article, stated: "Ayres thinks that the way farmers have cut down their maple groves is bad, their marketing worse. He would 1) bar anyone producing syrup outside of Vermont from calling it 'Vermont syrup'; 2) set up a state marketing and quality commission; 3) have packers take over the entire marketing program." Numerous articles also appeared in the *Rutland Herald* during 1947. A comment in the Cary Company records, made by manager A.B. Moore, tells the rest of the story:

Prices were discussed with the farmers at an open meeting before Governor Gibson and many objections were raised to the hairbrained suggestion of a retired Army Colonel, Fairfax Ayres, of Shaftsbury, over the low price of syrup in drums and the failure of our concern to take in all the farmers syrup, process it, merchandise it, and remit the profits to the farmers, deducting our costs. But this died down—the Colonel was invited over to see us and he paid us a visit, was given much information and passed out of the picture for the time being.

It is likely that the proposal Ayres made that Vermonters would have found most outlandish was his suggestion that they *stop eating their own maple syrup!* He did not think they could afford to consume their own product, not so long as they needed to use the proceeds "to buy a new plow point or improve their stock."

Ayres's scheming happened the year after the Office of Price Administration (OPA) ceiling on maple syrup was raised. Ayres was urging more, stating that he was getting fifteen dollars for syrup that he shipped to Europe. Rejected by most, his ideas provided some "food for thought" for maple farmers.

Making Much of Vermont Maple—Promoting the Green Mountain State's Signature Product

SUPERFINE MAPLE SYRUP
Put up in Square Gallon and Half-Gallon Cans and Bottles. MAPLE SUGAR Put up in 10 and 28 Pound Pails, also Large and Small Cakes. ORDER EARLY and the very best of goods will be secured. Premium was awarded us at the World's Fair.

    – E.L. Bass, West Randolph, Vermont; advertisement in
How to Procure Pure Vermont Maple Sugar and Syrup

Who can say when the promotion of Pure Vermont Maple Syrup really began? Imagine the Native Peoples, with sugar-laden makaks in canoes, promoting as they endeavored to trade!

The Move to Gain More Money from the Maple Crop

World's Fair premiums brought "bragging rights" that could be used in advertising. At the World's Fair in London in 1850, Vermonters exhibited maple sugar. "L. Dean of Manchester and W. Barnes were awarded medals for their Maple Sugar."[99] Those sugarmakers were aiming for the European market!

One of the earliest recorded instances of organized group promotion was the maple exhibit at the Chicago World's Fair of 1893, described in the eighth chapter of this book.

In 1894, one year after organizing, the Vermont Maple Sugarmakers' Association published a promotional booklet, *How to Procure Pure Vermont Maple Sugar and Syrup*. The booklet contained a history of maple production in Vermont, an explanation of labeling and Vermont laws relating to purity, a listing of the names and addresses of association members who "could be counted on to provide an unadulterated product," advertisements and thirty-six "receipts" for "Using Maple Sugar."

A poem urged careful consumerism:

MARY
As you are going to town
Please send or bring some syrup down,
Some Maple Syrup and 'twill be
Bottled and labeled you will see.

JOHN
Now, Mary, you don't want that stuff,
Of glucose we have had enough,
So this is what we'd better do,
Send to Vermont and get it new,
There you know laws are made,
Whereby adulterations are staid
And if you doubt the label's true,
Why, testing it will prove to you
That in this State one can be sure
That he will get it clear and pure—
The other States no fines impose,
Perhaps 'tis pure, the maker knows![100]

"The Vermont Special"—the Sugar Train

Vermont author Harriet Fletcher-Fisher wrote several news articles about a long-forgotten grand scheme to promote Vermont products. A train trip was organized in 1927 by the Central Vermont Railway. Cars with sixty-three exhibits were prepared at a number of places in Vermont, and gathered in Burlington, where seven Pullman cars for the passengers were added to the train. The total "Vermont Special" consisted of fourteen cars, hauling 134 passengers and exhibits. It was quickly dubbed the "Sugar Train." The trip took ten days, travelling from Burlington, through Washington, D.C., south to Columbia, South Carolina, west through Birmingham, Alabama, Memphis, Tennessee and Oklahoma City, then north to Omaha, Nebraska, then east through Chicago, Toronto and Montreal and south again to Burlington. Along the way, eighteen additional rail lines were used, all organized by the Central Vermont Railway. A news clipping mentioned the splendid diners (cars) added by the Canadian Pacific Railway in Toronto, taking the place of "the fine brace of feeders sent out from Des Moines to Chicago." The train at that point was sixteen cars long.

The delegation was led by Governor and Mrs. John Weeks, who added status to the mission. Other Vermonters aboard represented various industries and agencies. There were many stops along the way, when people had the opportunity to come aboard and see the displays of Vermont natural and manufactured products—maple sugar and candy from the Cary Company were featured, along with photographs of maple production. The scheduled stops provided opportunities for the Vermonters to present gifts to the mayors and officials of the various cities, and the travelers were royally hosted at banquets, sometimes three in a day. President Calvin Coolidge enjoyed a taste of maple from his home state when the group arrived at the White House. It was noted that many "ex-Vermonters" met the train at each stop—relatives and friends of those aboard, as well as homesick former residents of the Green Mountain State.

The Move to Gain More Money from the Maple Crop

The 1929 train left from Montpelier with two hundred people aboard and loaded with Vermont products, again led by Governor Weeks. A send-off dinner for the travelers was held at the Hotel Pavilion. Again, the train traveled south, west, north and east, drawing crowds of people and stopping for passengers to be entertained along the way. This time, it was President Herbert Hoover who greeted the group at the White House. The president conferred with Governor Weeks regarding Vermont's progress in recovery from the flood of 1927; he had visited the state following that disaster. Hoover congratulated Vermont on its recovery, "as indicated by the tour now being made." The president was presented with Vermont maple syrup "for his griddle cakes."

Also aboard the train in 1929 was Charles Walker, a reporter for the *Caledonian-Record* who telegraphed reports of the journey back to the paper and had copies of the paper shipped to the train. His accounts are a lasting record of a significant promotional effort,

Cary Company exhibit at the first Eastern States Exposition, 1929. *Courtesy of the New England Maple Museum.*

155

"the Sugar Train," a four-thousand-mile trip "Exhibiting Vermont Resources, Manufactured Products and Scenic Attractions."[101]

The "Big E"

The Vermont Legislature provided the Maple Sugarmakers' Association with an opportunity to showcase their products when the Vermont Building was constructed and opened in 1929 on the Avenue of States at the Eastern States Exposition in Springfield, Massachusetts. Each of the New England States maintains a facility at the Exposition, which is held annually in September. Perhaps learning from the negative experience of being dwarfed by larger buildings at the Chicago World's Fair of 1893, thirty-six years later the Legislators provided $60,500, enough funds for an impressive building, bearing external resemblance to the Vermont Statehouse in Montpelier. Thousands of visitors poured through the doors that year, purchasing their share of Pure Vermont Maple products, as they have continued to do annually.

The Vermont Farm Bureau and the First Vermont Maple Festival

Spring is the time for a maple celebration, and the right time to stage a promotional event to sell the new crop. In the January–February 1936 issue of the *Vermonter*, A. Richie Low wrote:

> *Because what potatoes mean to Maine, maple products mean to Vermont, the State Farm Bureau made up its mind to do something that would make the American people more maple syrup conscious…It was decided that one of the most effective ways to bring this about would be through the holding, on a state wide basis, of a maple festival. The date set was March 1st, 1935.*

Arthur Packard, president of the Farm Bureau and a chairman, together set up county organizations; the fourteen county chairs appointed leaders in the towns, who had charge of events that would happen in local festivals. About seventeen thousand people turned out to enjoy sugar-on-snow, dancing and card playing. "The festival did much to revive the kind of neighborliness our fathers and mothers enjoyed when they were young." The event also attracted the desired media attention:

> *The newspapers played a large part in making the maple sugar festival a success...The afternoon of the day the festival was held Governor Charles M. Smith delivered an address over the radio urging Vermonters to attend...Lieut-Gov. George Aiken journeyed to Schenectady, from which city he broadcast a message from WGY...Thus he reached not only those attending the festivals, but a great multitude of others who were tuned in. Because of this widespread publicity both in the press and over the air, men and women in New England and beyond came to learn of our state wide maple sugar festival.*[102]

An important feature of the festival was a cake-baking contest. "The cake...could be any kind of cake provided it had a maple sugar frosting." Twelve hundred cakes were entered! One winner was chosen in each county, and from those fourteen the top three were chosen. "The first two cake winners were given a trip to Washington, D.C." The first prize winner took her cake to the White House for the president's table, the second prize cake was delivered directly to the vice president and the third prize winner chose an airplane trip to Boston, where she presented her cake to Massachusetts Governor Curley.

The official Vermont Maple Festival of today is held annually in St. Albans at the end of April, and has been run by volunteers since its founding in the late 1960s.

ROLLING OUT THE RED CARPET—VERMONT'S *FIRST* SPECIALTY PRODUCT

Vermont sugarmakers "roll out the red carpet" for visitors! Many tourists travel to the Green Mountain State because of maple—for

Left: Three popular sugarhouses by the side of the road, attracting tourists: Green Mountain Sugarhouse, Ludlow; Dakin Farm, N. Ferrisburgh; and Harlow's Sugarhouse, Putney.

Opposite, top: The von Trapp family gathering sap. *Courtesy of the Trapp Family Lodge.*

Opposite, bottom: The von Trapp family sugar-on-snow party, 1943. *Courtesy of the Trapp Family Lodge.*

the taste of new syrup in spring celebrations, the glorious color of the maple leaves during fall foliage, the fairs, festivals and field days where they can enjoy maple creemees (Vermont word for soft ice cream), maple cotton candy and maple sugar-on-snow that cannot be shipped! Maple has been Vermont's signature product since the time of the Native Peoples.

Sugarhouses arrived at the roadside! During the first half of the twentieth century, farmers began to realize that tourists wanted to see maple sugaring and bring home maple goodies directly from a sugarhouse. Visitors wanted to meet the sugarmaker and have a personal experience. Most sugarhouses were located in the woods, and negotiating off-roads during "mud season" was chancy. So sugarhouses began to be moved or built by the side of paved roads, where steam coming from the cupolas signaled a sweet invitation, and retail shops were ready to satisfy the needs of visitors.

The von Trapp family created a tourist destination, and also took to sugarmaking when they came to America! One of their "Sounds of Music" was the "plink" "plunk" of sap dripping in buckets! When

The Move to Gain More Money from the Maple Crop

Georg and Maria von Trapp arrived in the United States with their family in 1942, they made their home on a 660-acre farm in Stowe. The farm had a sugarbush and a working sugarhouse. The Trapps went about producing maple syrup, canning it and labeling it as their own "Trapp Family Farm Pure Vermont Maple Syrup." The Trapp Family Lodge continues to offer tourists a traditional maple sugaring experience in their modern sugarhouse.

Above, left: Martina von Trapp labeling syrup cans. *Courtesy of the Trapp Family Lodge.*

Above, right: Elaborate labels designed to attract purchasers. *Courtesy of Special Collections, Bailey-Howe Library, University of Vermont.*

Below: Lithographs replaced paper labels on containers.

The Move to Gain More Money from the Maple Crop

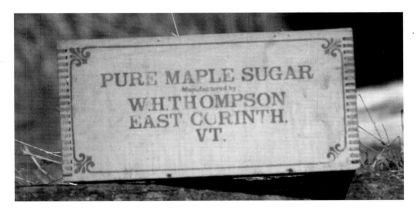

Above: Maple sugar boxes shipped sugar "away."

Left: Wooden book-shaped candy box, embossed with "The Sweetest Story Ever Told By A Maple Tree Published by Mount Mansfield Merchants, Stowe, Vermont."

Sugarmakers found that pretty packaging promoted Pure Vermont Maple. When syrup gained in popularity over maple sugar, plain rectangular metal containers, affixed with paper labels, were used by most farmers. Later, lithographed containers brightened the packaging with pictures of sugaring scenes, and elaborate labels were designed to make products stand out in the marketplace. Wooden boxes for shipping sugar protected the contents, and some wooden "book" boxes were special containers for candy or block sugar.

Chapter 15

Tools of the Trade

Sugarmakers know how to tinker, and use what they have on the farm to produce maple syrup.
— *David Marvin, son of maple researcher James Marvin*

Bygone Tools From Yesteryear

Early sugarmaker tools have a story to tell. The sugar "devil," or sugar auger, is one of the most captivating. During the major part of the 1800s and early 1900s, farmers made hard sugar, which was put up in wooden barrels held together by iron hoops. Most folks were impeccably honest in trading. However, there were the unscrupulous, dishonest sellers who added rocks to the bottom of the barrels to increase weight. The sugar devil, with its sharp center prong and wickedly curved outer prongs, was a multipurpose tool; it could readily break up the hard sugar into smaller chunks for more convenient use, *or* it could be screwed right down to the bottom of the barrel, checking for illicit material—helpful to wary country store owners!

When a large chunk of sugar was brought to the table, sugar nippers could be used to chip off small bits to sweeten food and drink. They are more delicate and refined than the tools intended for kitchen work.

Another tool useful for breaking up hard chunks was the sugar pick, a miniature version of a miner's pick. Smaller in size and

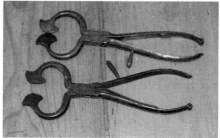

Left: A sugar devil, an antique sugar tool.

Above: Sugar nippers, an antique table tool.

lighter in weight, lacking the screwing force of the sugar devil, it was most appropriate for the pantry. When a chunk could be chopped from the hard mass of sugar, the maker of the pie, cake or preserves of corn mush could then use a knife to shave maple sugar from the chunk.

In the attic of an old Vermont farmhouse, Bill and Marie Danforth of Tunbridge found a box of curious items that could not be identified by any of the sugarmakers to whom the gadgets were shown. Then Marie found an advertisement in a 1921 issue of a farm magazine. There it was—"the sap chaser." The ad told how it was used. A small galvanized metal tube could be slipped over the end of each spout, with two or three tubes running sap into one bucket. Bill explains: "It saved on buckets, but you'd have to gather more often, because the bucket would fill up more quickly."

The settler sugarmakers had few conveniences, particularly when it came to gathering sap. In addition to snowshoes, perhaps the greatest convenience for collecting was the shoulder yoke and gathering pail. Shoulder yokes could be made right on the farm, hollowed from logs, to roughly fit the shoulders of the wearer. The yokes spread the heavy weight of buckets of sap over the shoulders of the person collecting. Shoulder yokes and gathering pails were also used to bring water from a spring, or milk from the barn.

Right: A sugar pick, an antique pantry tool.

Below: A shoulder yoke and gathering pail—two pails, wider at the bottom than the top to avoid spillage, would hang from the yoke. *Courtesy of the Coombs Collection.*

The earliest candy molds were carved from wood, both by the Native Peoples and the settlers. In the late nineteenth and early twentieth centuries, square and rectangular wooden molds were used to make sugar cakes—one pound, two pound and more. Elaborate molds were carved from wood to form three-dimensional hard sugar cakes in the shape of houses, sugarhouses and churches. A bottom piece and four sides fitted together, and were secured by a wooden brace.

Antique wooden sugarhouse mold, with a base, three sides and a brace, makes a three-dimensional hard sugar "house."

Metal molds, assorted shapes and sizes.

Mold with multiple divisions for small candies. *Courtesy of the Coombs Collection.*

With the availability of metal, individual molds became popular. Candy was made for home use and for sale. The earliest molds were flat-bottomed; later shapes became more intricate. Some featured in the collection pictured were made in the shape of sap buckets. Many were heart shaped, or scalloped. Others were tiny, possibly dollhouse toys. Metal molds in the form of racks with multiple metal divisions were used in factories, or in sugarhouses where small, plain candies were produced for sale.

W.C. Brower patented a metal pipeline in 1916. The system seemed like an answer to a sugarmaker's prayer, designed to bring the sap right down to the sugarhouse without slogging through the snow. Unfortunately, the system did not work well. Ice, snow, deer and other animals caused it to break apart.

MORE TOOLS FROM YESTERYEAR—STILL IN USE TODAY!

A time-honored tool, the sugarmakers' scoop, is widely used today (in addition to all the high-tech tools available) to test boiling sap for approximate syrup readiness. When the scoop is dipped into

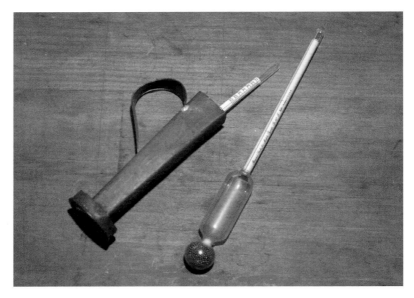

Antique hydrometers for measuring sugar content; both sap (in the cup) and syrup hydrometer are shown.

the liquid and held aloft, if an "apron" or "sheet" forms along the straight bottom edge, then the sugarmaker knows that it's just about the correct legal density. (See no. 5 on the image on page 138 for the scoop and skimmer.)

The skimmer is similar to a scoop in shape, but with perforations or a metal screen making up most of the center portion of the scoop. It is a tool useful for skimming off foam, or floating impurities that may accumulate throughout the boiling process prior to filtering, which is the final step in assuring the required-by-law absolutely clear syrup.

One of the instruments that is used to measure sugar content is the hydrometer. Available in versions for both sap and syrup, they are immersed in sap or syrup in a tall cup. The hydrometer floats with a weighted ball, exhibiting calibrations that indicate percentages of sugar content.

Evaporators are the most central tools to production in the sugarhouse. There is no authenticated record of the *first* use of an

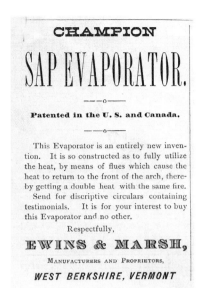

Champion Evaporator advertisement. *Courtesy of George Ewins.*

evaporator in Vermont. Considering the tendency of Vermonters to tinker and invent, there was probably an evaporator in use, albeit a flat pan, before anyone wrote about it. Suggestions for construction of flat pans were made as early as the late 1700s. Flat pans are described as similar to giant metal cake pans, sometimes four feet wide and six feet long.

W.C. Alvord mentions having an evaporator in Wilmington, Vermont, in 1862. H. Allen Soule, a Vermont inventor, describes an evaporator design in 1872. Soule's design would later become the King Evaporator, still in use in some sugarhouses today. Eventually the King Evaporator was manufactured by the Leader Evaporator Company, which still incorporates some elements of the King Evaporator in their newest designs.

In the 1882–83 *Gazetteer and Business Directory of Franklin and Grand Isle Counties, VT,* Philo Ewins and his partner, a Mr. Marsh, were advertising the Champion Sap Evaporator, patented in the United States of America and Canada: "It is so constructed as to fully utilize the heat, by means of flues which cause the heat to return to the front of the arch, thereby getting a double heat from the same

Ceramic Grimm company jug, an unusual one-third of a gallon in size.

fire." According to George Ewins, descendant of Philo, there was a Champion factory in West Berkshire that is no longer in existence.

The G.H. Grimm Company, then located in Hudson, Ohio, patented their evaporator in 1884. In 1890, the company moved to Rutland, Vermont, where they also manufactured maple utensils, and marketed syrup under their own label. Somewhat perplexing is the fact that by 1904, and thereafter, G.H. Grimm was advertising the Champion Evaporator, the same name that was advertised by Ewins and Marsh in 1882. Did Grimm purchase the patent from Ewins and Marsh? History to be investigated!

Designs for evaporators that would increase the flow of sap from entry to the syrup point, or would speed the evaporation process due to greater exposure to heat sources, competed vigorously with each other. Particularly notable was the Leader drop flue pan, with corrugations reaching down into the fire. By 1888, the Leader Evaporator Company was manufacturing evaporators and sugaring tools. Founded in Enosburg Falls, they later relocated to Burlington, thereafter to St. Albans and then Swanton.

The Lightning Evaporator was manufactured in Richford. It is told that an iron foundry in which the Lightning had originally

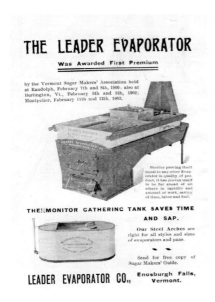

THE LEADER EVAPORATOR

Was Awarded First Premium

by the Vermont Sugar Makers' Association held at Randolph, February 7th and 8th, 1900; also at Burlington, Vt., February 5th and 6th, 1902; Montpelier, February 11th and 12th, 1903.

Besides proving itself equal to any other Evaporator in quality of product, it has proven itself to be far ahead of all others in rapidity and amount of work, saving of time, labor and fuel.

THE MONITOR GATHERING TANK SAVES TIME AND SAP.

Our Steel Arches are right for all styles and sizes of evaporators and pans.

Send for free copy of Sugar Makers' Guide.

LEADER EVAPORATOR CO., Enosburgh Falls, Vermont.

Leader Evaporator advertisement from a 1904 booklet.

been made was washed away in the flood of 1927, and operations were moved to another Richford building. An advertisement for the Lightning Evaporator features Noah Fleury, "Maple Sugar King"—the 1949 winner of the first statewide award for maple production excellence. This evaporator is still in use by Noah Fleury's family.

Another Vermont company patented the Bellows Falls Evaporator in 1891. By 1909, and possibly earlier, a Monarch Evaporator was being manufactured in Newport.

Evaporators were manufactured in other states and in Canada, but Vermont claimed a good share of the evaporator business! One must conclude that the number of evaporator manufacturers in the Green Mountain State is attributable to the intense interest of Vermonters in all aspects of maple production and to their tendency to "tinker." The only two Vermont companies that have lasted over time are Grimm and Leader. Now merged, they continue the tradition of fine craftsmanship, and are among the preeminent suppliers of evaporators and accessories for "maple people" in Vermont, other United States maple regions and Canada.

171

Chapter 16

Old-Time Maple "Receipts"

I eat my peas with syrup,
I've done it all my life.
It makes my peas taste funny,
But it keeps them on my knife!
— Author Unknown

Vermont Sugar-On-Snow (Jack Wax)

What is the most historic Vermont maple recipe? Probably sugar-on-snow, dating back to the Native Peoples, popular with the settlers who held "sugaring off" parties and still a treat found at most Vermont celebrations!

1 quart Pure Vermont Maple Syrup
Packed clean snow or well-crushed ice

Rub the rim of the pot with butter or cooking oil. Heat the syrup over medium heat, watching the pot; turn heat down if it threatens to boil over. When a candy thermometer reaches about 234°, or the syrup is at the "soft ball" stage, remove from the heat. Test by dribbling tablespoon of syrup over the snow. If the syrup sits on top of the snow and clings to a fork like taffy, it's ready. Pour in "ribbons" over snow packed in bowls.

Currier and Ives, *Forest Scene*, a view of sugaring in 1855 that also depicts a sugar-on-snow party.

Traditionally served with sour pickles and plain doughnuts—"A forkful of maple taffy, a bite of pickle to 'cut the sweet,' a bite of doughnut, and repeat!"

VERMONT MAPLE BAKED BEANS

The best baked beans you'll ever taste!

2 pounds dried beans, yellow eye, navy or soldier
½ pound lean salt pork (optional, or substitute bacon equivalent)
½ teaspoon baking soda
1 teaspoon salt
1 teaspoon dry mustard
1 medium-sized onion, peeled
1½–2 cups (depending on sweetness preferred) Pure Vermont Maple Syrup, dark is best
½ cup catsup

174

Wash and pick over beans. Cover with cold water, add soda and soak overnight. In the morning rinse beans and boil gently in fresh water until skins wrinkle. Drain off bean water and retain. Preheat oven to 325°. Place onion in the bottom of the bean pot or casserole. Add remaining ingredients that have been gently mixed. Place pork or bacon on top. Pour in bean water just to cover. Bake, covered, for about 8 hours. Check periodically, adding bean water as needed. For the last hour, cook uncovered to brown top.

VERMONT MAPLE BAKED HAM

1 ham, any size
1 cup Pure Vermont Maple Syrup for each 5 pounds of ham
1½ cups ham drippings
1½ cups water
4½ tablespoons flour
Bake ham with about ¾ cup of water in pan until partially done. This is about half of the cooking time. Remove the 1½ cups of drippings from pan for gravy. Cover ham with maple syrup, continue to bake ham covered, basting frequently, until done according to meat thermometer. To make gravy: blend flour into drippings, add water, bring to a boil, cook until thickened. (Note: Some Vermont hams now can be purchased fully cooked. In that case, baste with maple syrup as you warm, according to directions.)

MAPLE PUDDING CAKE

1½ cups unbleached white flour
2 teaspoons baking powder
¾ cup of milk
¾ cup of water
2 tablespoons butter
¾ cup maple or white sugar

Maple Sugarin' in Vermont

¼ teaspoon salt
1½ cups Pure Vermont Maple Syrup

Preheat oven to 350°. Combine flour, sugar, baking powder and salt. Stir in milk. Spread batter in a 9" greased baking pan or dish. Combine syrup, water and butter in saucepan and heat, until butter is melted. Gently pour the heated liquid over batter in the pan and bake about 45 minutes until cake is lightly browned. The maple syrup mixture will sink to the bottom where it forms a pudding-like sauce. Cool briefly, and top with whipped cream or ice cream.

Vermont Maple Griddlecakes or Waffles

Not difficult, and better than any mix!

2 cups unbleached all-purpose flour (such as King Arthur)
2 tablespoons sugar
1½ teaspoons baking powder
½ teaspoon baking soda
2 eggs
2 cups butter milk or sour milk (add 4 tablespoons vinegar or lemon juice to sweet milk and let stand to clabber)
½ cup melted butter or vegetable oil
Pure Vermont Maple Syrup

Mix dry ingredients thoroughly. Beat the eggs and buttermilk together. Add the butter or oil. Blend wet and dry ingredients lightly. Grease griddle or waffle iron and preheat. The griddle is ready when a drop of water "dances" on it. Pour batter onto griddle leaving room for expansion. Turn when bubbles form on top. If preparing waffles, follow directions for your waffle iron. Have your syrup pitcher filled to the brim!

Historically Vermonters have been known for using maple syrup creatively—on grapefruit, in oatmeal, coffee, tea—in a host of products.

Victorian pitcher of fancy syrup.

VERMONT SUGARMAKERS FAVORITE DESSERT!

Vanilla ice cream
Pure Vermont Maple Syrup (can be warmed briefly to thicken)

Pour the syrup over the ice cream. That's it!

One of Vermont Sugarmakers' required skills is the ability to taste and evaluate flavor to grade their syrup. And they use this skill on other occasions! At banquets and sugarmaker celebrations, where this recipe is almost always served as dessert, spoons are not immediately dug into the ice cream. It's an education for a non-sugarmaker to watch as spoons ladle up a little syrup, which is slowly and carefully tasted, savoring the flavor, evaluating, before the dessert is enjoyed.

Bill Godfrey's Famous Maple Candy—in His Own Words

Boil one quart of Fancy maple syrup to 233°. Take the pot off, and put the pot into cold water for 15 minutes. Then stir it like the devil! Then drop spoonfuls onto waxed paper. Put a fancy pecan on each one, fast before they cool.

More Vermont maple recipes, both "old time" and "nouvelle cuisine," can be found in *The Vermont Maple Festival Cookbook* (www.vtmaplefestival.org) and *The Official Vermont Maple Cookbooks*, second and third editions (www.vtmaple.org).

Old Leader company spout with a drip of sap sparkling in the sun.

Appendix

Recommended Resources

WEBSITES
Proctor Maple Research Center. www.edu/~pmrc
University of Vermont Extension. www.uvm.edu/~uvmaple
Vermont Agency of Agriculture. www.vtagriculture.com
Vermont Agency of Tourism. www.vermontvacation.com
Vermont Maple Festival. www.vtmaplefestival.com
Vermont Maple Sugarmakers' Association. www.vtmaple.org

BOOKS
Sweet Maple—James Lawrence
The Maple Sugar Book—Helen and Scott Nearing
Sweet Days and Beyond—Burr Morse
*The Maple Sugaring Story: A Guide to Teaching and Learning about the Maple
Industry*—Perceptions, Inc.

VIDEOS
Available at www.perceptionsvermont.com:
The Maple Sugaring Story
Voices from the Sugarwoods
Proud Tradition: Pure Vermont Maple

SOME VERMONT PLACES TO VISIT
New England Maple Museum, Pittsford (seasonal)
Shelburne Farms, Shelburne
Green Mountain Audubon Society, Huntington (seasonal)
Maple Grove, St. Johnsbury
Abenaki Tribal Museum, Swanton
Trapp Family Lodge, Stowe
Rokeby Museum, N. Ferrisburgh (Underground Railroad) (seasonal)
Shelburne Museum, Shelburne (seasonal)
Billings Farm Museum, Woodstock

PARTIAL LIST OF VERMONT SUGARHOUSES AND SHOPS; PLACES TO ASK QUESTIONS AND LEARN MORE ABOUT MAPLE
Green Mountain Sugarhouse, Ludlow
Harlow's Sugarhouse, Putney (seasonal)
Dakin Farm, N. Ferrisburgh
Vermont Maple Outlet, Jeffersonville
Bragg Farm, East Montpelier
Morse Farm, Montpelier
Goodrich's Maple Farm, Cabot
Butternut Mountain Farm Shop, Johnson
Couture's Maple Shop, Westfield
Many more are listed on www.vermontagriculture.com and www.vtmaple.org. Some are seasonal.

Notes

INTRODUCTION:

1. Everett Willard, in the video *Pure Vermont Maple: A Proud Tradition.*
2. Many of the earliest quotes used, although authentic, may be attributable to Native Peoples outside the region of the Abenaki Peoples of the Dawnland. It is surmised that the similarities are greater than the differences, because it is generally known that many customs were similar and shared among the Native Peoples. Since this is not an exploration of a single historical event but rather of a cultural lifestyle practice that occurred and evolved over time, it may be inferred that earlier history is reflected in some of the quotes.

CHAPTER 1:

3. Nicholas Denys, *Histoire naturelle des Peuples des Animaux, des Arbres et Plantes de l'Amerique Septentrionale*, in Helen and Scott Nearing's *The Maple Sugar Book*, 22.
4. Fred H. Taylor, former chair of the Vermont Maple History Committee, in a note to the author.
5. Lee Sultzman, "Abenaki Location." www.tolatsga.org/aben.html.
6. Frederick Wiseman, "Abenaki," *The Vermont Encyclopedia*, ed. John J. Duffy, Samual B. Hand, and Ralph H. Orth, 31.
7. Signage at the Abenaki Tribal Museum in Swanton, Vermont.
8. Wiseman, "Abenaki."
9. William A. Haviland and Marjory W. Power, *The Original Vermonters: Native Inhabitants Past and Present*, 152.
10. Ibid., 149.
11. C. Keith Wilbur, *The New England Indians*, 35.
12. Ibid.
13. W.J. Hoffman. *14th Annual Report of the Bureau of Ethnology*, 288, found in Nearing's *Maple Sugar Book*, 31.
14. Information supplied by Swanton Abenaki Aaron York.
15. Christine "Cookie" Barrett, telephone interview.
16. Haviland and Powers, *Original Vermonters*, 159.
17. Nearing, *Maple Sugar Book*, 29.
18. Fred Taylor, personal note.

19. Harmon Morse, *Vermont Agriculture Report of 1889–1890*, 85.

20. Frances Densmore, *How Indians Used Wild Plants for Food, Medicine and Crafts*, 312. Originally located in the *44th Annual Report of the Bureau of Ethnology, Smithsonian Institution, 1926–1928*, United States Government Printing Office, 1928.

21. Rowland E. Robinson, "Old Time Sugar-Making," *The Atlantic Monthly*, 467–68.

22. Michael J. Caduto and Joseph Bruchac, *Keepers of the Earth*, 145.

23. James Lawrence and Rux Martin, *Sweet Maple*, 55–56.

24. Patrick J. Munson, "Still More on the Antiquity of Maple Sugar and Syrup in Aboriginal Eastern North America," *Journal of Ethnobiology* 9, 158–71.

25. Marc Lescarbot, *Histoire de la nouvelle France*, in Nearing's *Maple Sugar Book*, 22.

26. Paul Le Jeune, *Nouvelle France en l'enée*, in Nearing's *Maple Sugar Book*, 22.

27. Alexander Henry, *Travels and Adventures in Canada and the Indian Territories, between the Years 1760–1776*, 70. Also found in Nearing's *Maple Sugar Book*, 36.

28. Peter Kalm, "Dissertation for the Royal Sweden Academy of Sciences," 155. Also found in Nearing's *Maple Sugar Book*, 36.

29. Benjamin Rush, *An Account of the Sugar Maple Tree of the United States*, in Nearing's *Maple Sugar Book*, 36.

30. George Catlin, *Letters and Notes on the Manners, Customs and Conditions of the North American Indians*, 98, in Nearing's *Maple Sugar Book*, 38.

31. Henry B. Schoolcraft, *Indian Tribes of the United States*, 199, in Nearing's *Maple Sugar Book*, 27.

32. C. Keith Wilbur, *The New England Indians*, 34.

33. Densmore, *How Indians Used*, 312–13.

34. Ibid.

35. Randall Heiligmann, Melvin Koelling, Timothy Perkins, eds., *North American Maple Syrup Manual*, 292.

36. Ibid.

37. Ibid.

38. Pehr Kalm, "Dissertation."

39. Densmore, *How Indians Used*, 312.

40. Ibid., 313.

CHAPTER 2:

41. Wm. J. Watson, Esq., *The Emigrant's Guide to the Canadas*, http://freepages.genealogy.rootsweb.com/~wjmartin/emig1822.htm.

42. Evans, Francis A., Esq. *The Emigrant's Directory and Guide*, 105.

43. Originally named New Connecticut, the name was changed in 1777, adapted from the French—"Verd-Mont"—meaning Green Mountain, to the more easily said "Vermont." Cora Cheney, *Vermont: The State with the Storybook Past*, 68.

44. Miller, "Journal of James Whitelaw," *History of Ryegate*.

45. Abby Maria Hemenway, *Historical Gazetteer* vol. 1, 313.

46. Zadock Thompson, *History of the State of Vermont*, 58.

47. Samuel Williams, *The Natural and Civil History of Vermont*, 364.

48. There are two dates for Alexander Kathan's Bible—one 1775 noted in Hall's *History of Eastern Vermont*, and one in the same volume, containing notes (dated 1761) of the type usually contained in a Bible. The 1761 date is more likely accurate since it tells of his arrival to Fulham (later Putney) on May 1, 1761.

49. Benjamin Hall, *History of Eastern Vermont*, 108–9.

50. "Molasses" is a settler term for maple syrup.

51. Abby Maria Hemenway, *Abby Maria Hemenway's Vermont, Selected and Edited by Brenda C. Morrissey*, 75.

52. David Mansfield, *History of the Kathan Family*, 4, 128.

53. Watson, *Emigrant's Guide*.

54. Cheney, *Vermont*.

55. Samuel Williams, *Weather Diary 1791*, Vermont Historical Society; the *Vermont Gazette*, February 28, April 4, April 11 and April 25, 1791; David Ludlum, *The Vermont Weather Book*, 254–56. Weather record analysis by Mark Breen, meteorologist at Fairbanks Museum in St. Johnsbury.

CHAPTER 3:

56. The Thomas Jefferson Papers, Monticello.

57. Edmund Burke, *Annual Register, Useful Projects*.

58. This and preceding references to Thomas Jefferson are from the maple sugar collection of his papers at Monticello.

CHAPTER 4:

59. Howard Russell, *A Long Deep Furrow*, 96–97.

60. J.A. Graham, *A Descriptive Sketch*.

61. Williams, *Natural and Civil History of Vermont*.

62. Nathan Hoskins, *A History of the State of Vermont*, 17, 271–72.

63. Solon Robinson, *Facts for Farmers*, 837.

64. Ibid.

65. Ibid.

66. Russell, *Long Deep Furrow*, 171.

CHAPTER 5:

67. C.T. Alvord, *The Manufacture of Maple Sugar* in the *First Agricultural Report of the U.S. Department of Agriculture*, 394–405.

CHAPTER 6:

68. Marty Sprague, "Adams and Haynes Overview."

69. "The Anti-Slavery Movement," www.vermonthistory.org.

70. Clarence Porter Cowles, "The Early History of Maple Sugar," *The Vermonter*, 107.

71. The Thomas Jefferson Papers.

72. Walter Crockett, *Vermont: The Green Mountain State*, 332.

73. Ibid., 335.

CHAPTER 7:

74. Margaret MacArthur, "Maple Sweet," *An Almanac of New England Farm Songs.*

75. Illustration found on page 96 clearly depicts a draw tub rig for gathering sap.

76. E.A. Fiske, *Second Report of the Vermont Board of Agriculture, Manufactures & Mining,* 711–24.

CHAPTER 8:

77. "Maple Sugar," *Twelfth Report of the Vermont Board of Agriculture, 1891–1892,* 334.

78. "Maple Sugar," *Twelfth, Thirteenth, Fourteenth, Fifteenth* and *Sixteenth Report of the Vermont Board of Agriculture, 1891, 1892, 1893, 1894* and *1895.*

79. *Thirteenth Report,* 1893.

80. H.H. McIntyre, *1893–94 State Agriculture Board Report,* 238–58.

CHAPTER 9:

81. Victor I. Spear in *Fifteenth* and *Sixteenth Agricultural Report,* 31–41.

82. Perry Chase and A.R. Phillips, *Twelfth Annual Meeting, Vermont Maple Sugar Makers' Assoc.,* 8–20.

83. Redfield Proctor correspondence, Proctor Vermont Library.

CHAPTER 10:

84. "Mud Season" is the time between late February and mid-April when the frost leaves the ground, and unpaved roads present problems for travel. It was a time when school vacations were frequently declared.

85. Lois Greer, "America's Maple Sugar King: George C. Cary," *The Vermonter* 4, no. 1, January 1919, 3–8.

86. *Cary Maple Sugar,* 35 mm film, Phillipe Beaudry Collection, Northeast Historic Film, Bucksport, Maine.

87. Unpublished paper for the Vermont Maple History Committee, Edward "Sherb" Doubleday, 1990, and found in the Cary Collection at the New England Maple Museum.

CHAPTER 11:

88. "Maple Sugar," *Bulletin 26, Vermont State Agricultural Experiment Station* (Burlington: Free Press Association, 1891).

89. Mary Lighthall, "C.H.," Unpublished paper.

90. Fred Taylor, interview.

CHAPTER 12:

91. E.H. Jones, *Twentieth Report.* 15.

92. Ray Foulds, interview.

93. Lucien Paquette, interview.

CHAPTER 13:

94. Crockett, *Vermont.* 135.

95. Crockett, *Vermont*. 367.

96. E.H. Jones, *Twentieth Biennial Report, Commissioner of Agriculture, 1939–1940*, 15.

97. From Wilson "Bill" Clark's scrapbook and newspaper clippings, 1945.

98. Evelyn Stanley, *History of Enosburg.*

CHAPTER 14:

99. Crockett, *Vermont*, 394.

100. "How to Procure Vermont Maple Sugar and Syrup," *Vermont Maple Sugar Makers' Association*, 4.

101. Harriet Fletcher-Fisher, "Sugar Train," *The Independent*, April 5, 2000, and *The Caledonian-Record*, spring, 1994, supplement.

102. A. Ritchie Low, "Vt. Maple Festival," *The Vermonter*, 23–24.

Bibliography

Alvord, C.T. *The Manufacture of Maple Sugar*. United States Report of the Commissioner of Agriculture, 1863.

Bailey, L.H. *'Cyclopedia of American Agriculture*, volume II—Crops. New York: Macmillan Company, 1907.

Barratt, Christine "Cookie." 2008. Interview conducted by Betty Ann Lockhart.

Burke, Edmund. *Annual Register, Useful Projects*. Philadelphia: Society of Gentlemen, 1790.

Burlington Free Press. "Proceedings of the Vermont Maple Sugarmakers' Meeting." January 6, 1904.

Caduto, Michael J., and Joseph Bruchac. *Keepers of the Earth*. Golden, Colorado: Fulcrum, Inc., 1988.

Cary Maple Sugar Company. Unpublished papers, 1902–66. Collection of New England Maple Museum.

Cary Maple Sugar Company Film. Beaudry Collection of Northeast Historic Film, 1927.

Catlin, George. *Letters and Notes on the Manners, Customs and Conditions of the North American Indians*. Philadelphia: Hazard, 1857. Found in Helen Nearing's *The Maple Sugar Book*. New York: Schocken Books, 1950.

Chase, Perry, and A.R. Phillips. *Twelfth Annual Meeting, Vermont Maple Sugar Makers' Assoc.* St. Albans: Messenger, 1905.

Cheney, Cora. *Vermont: The State with the Storybook Past*. Brattleboro: The Stephen Greene Press, 1976.

Cowles, Clarence Porter. "The Early History of Maple Sugar." *The Vermonter*. March 1902.

Crockett, Walter. *Vermont: The Green Mountain State*. New York: The Century Book Company, 1921.

Densmore, Frances. *How Indians Used Wild Plants for Food, Medicine & Crafts*. New York: Dover Publications, 1974. First published in the *Forty-fourth Annual Report of the Bureau of American Ethnology, 1926–1927*.

BIBLIOGRAPHY

Denys, Nicholas. *Histoire naturelle des Peuples des Animaux, des Arbres et Plantes de l'Amerique Septentrionale, 1672.* Edited and translated by William F. Ganong. Toronto: Champlain Society, 1908. Nearing.

Doubleday, Edward. Unpublished paper for the Vermont Maple History Committee. Fred Laing, Chair.

Evans, Francis A. *The Emigrant's Directory and Guide to Obtain Lands and Effect A Settlement in the Canadas.* Dublin: William Curry, Jun. and Co., 1833.

Fiske, E.A. *Second Report of the Vermont Board of Agriculture, Manufactures & Mining.* Montpelier: Freeman Steam, 1874.

Fletcher-Fisher, Harriet. "Maple Train." *The Independent*, April 5, 2000, and *Caledonian-Record*, spring, 1994. Supplement.

Fox, William, and William Hubbard. *The Maple Sugar Industry.* Washington: Government Printing Office, 1905.

Gookin, Daniel. *Account of the Indians.* Boston: Massachusetts Historical Society, 1792.

Graham, J.A. *A Descriptive Sketch of the Present State of Vermont One of the United States of Americas, Letters to the Duke of Montrose.* London: self-published, 1797.

Hall, Benjamin. *History of Eastern Vermont.* New York: Appleton and Co., 1858.

Haviland, William A., and Marjory W. Power. *The Original Vermonters: Native Inhabitants Past and Present.* Published for the University of Vermont. Hanover: University Press of New England, 1981.

Heiligmann, Randall, Melvin Koelling, and Timothy Perkins, eds. *North American Maple Syrup Manual, Second Edition.* Columbus: Ohio State University, 2006.

Hemenway, Abby Maria. *Abby Maria Hemenway's Vermont, Selected and Edited by Brenda C. Morrissey.* Brattleboro: Stephen Greene Press, 1972.

Hemenway, Abby Maria. "Dummerston, Putney." *Historical Gazetteer* vol. V. Burlington, VT: Miss A.M. Hemenway, [etc.], 1891.

Henry, Alexander. *Travels and Adventures in Canada and the Indian Territories.* New York: Riley, 1809. Nearing.

Hoffman, W.J. *14th Annual Report of the Bureau of Ethnology.* Federal Publication. Washington, D.C.: 1896. Nearing.

Hoskins, Nathan. *A History of the State of Vermont: From Its Discovery and Settlement to the Close of the YEAR MDCCCXXX.* Vergennes: J. Shedd, 1831.

Kalm, Peter. "Dissertation for the Royal Swedish Academy of Sciences," 1751. Nearing.

Lawrence, James, and Rux Martin. *Sweet Maple.* Shelburne, Vermont: Chapters Publishing, 1993.

Lighthall, Mary. "C.H." Unpublished paper, 1972.

Low, A. Ritchie. "Vt. Maple Festival." *The Vermonter*, January 1936.

Ludlum, David. *The Vermont Weather Book.* Barre: The Vermont Historical Society, 1987.

Lufkin, Daniel. "History of Windham County." *Historical Gazetteer*, vol. V. Burlington, VT: Miss A.M. Hemenway, [etc.], 1891.

MacArthur, Margaret. *An Almanac of New England Farm Songs.* Green Linnet, B00005YQ99. Audiocassette. 1993.

Mansfield, David. *History of the Kathan Family*. Brattleboro: E.L. Hildreth & Co., 1902.

McIntyre, H.H. *1893–94 State Agriculture Board Report*. Burlington: Free Press Assoc., 1894.

Miller, Edward, and Frederic P. Wells. "James Whitelaw's Journal." *History of Ryegate, Vermont*. St. Johnsbury, VT: The Caledonian Company, 1913.

Morse, Burr. *Sweet Days and Beyond*. Poultney, Vermont: Historical Pages Company, 2005.

Morse, Harmon. *Vermont Agriculture Report of 1889–1890*. Montpelier, VT: Department of Agriculture, Argus and Patriot, 1890.

Munson, Patrick J. *Journal of Ethnobiology* 9, no. 2 (Winter 1989).

Nearing, Helen and Scott. *The Maple Sugar Book*. New York: Schocken Books, 1950.

Proctor, Redfield. Unpublished Letters and Papers. Library in Proctor, Vermont.

Robinson, Rowland E. "Old Time Sugar-Making." *The Atlantic Monthly*, April 1897.

Robinson, Solon. *Facts for Farmers*. New York: A.J. Johnson, 1869.

Rush, Benjamin. *An Account of the Sugar Maple Tree of the United States*. Philadelphia: Aitken, 1792.

Russell, Howard. *A Long Deep Furrow*. Hanover: University Press of New England, 1982.

Schoolcraft, Henry B. *Indian Tribes of the United States*. Philadelphia: Lippincott, 1884.

Sprague, Marty. "Adams and Haynes Overview." *Windham County Maplerama, 1992*. VT: Windham County Maple Producers, 1992.

Stanley, Evelyn. "The Maple Industry of Enosburgh." *History of Enosburgh, Vermont*.

Sultzman, Lee. "Abenaki Location." www.tolatsga.org/aben.html.

Taylor, Fred H. The Vermont Maple History Committee. Unpublished notes to the author.

The Thomas Jefferson Papers. Monticello, Charlottesville, Virginia.

Thompson, Zadock. *History of the State of Vermont*. Edward Smith, 1833.

Time. "Sugar Time." March 31, 1947.

Vermont Board of Agriculture. *Twelfth, Thirteenth, Fourteenth, Fifteenth* and *Sixteenth Reports 1891, 1892, 1893, 1894* and *1895*. Burlington, VT: Free Press Association and St. Albans, VT: Messenger Print.

Vermont Gazette (aka *Haswell's Vermont Gazette*), February 28, April 4, April 11 and April 25, 1791.

The Vermont Historical Society. "The Anti-Slavery Movement." www.vermonthistory.org

Vermont Maple Sugarmakers' Association booklet for 1894. South Royalton: Vermont Maple Sugarmakers' Association, 1894.

Vermont State Experimental Station Bulletin No. 26, Third Edition. Burlington, VT: Free Press Association, 1891.

Walker, Charles. "Let's Talk it Over." *Caledonian-Record*, April 1929.

Watson, William. *The Emigrant's Guide to the Canadas*. Dublin: G. Bull, 1822.

BIBLIOGRAPHY

Wilbur, C. Keith. *The New England Indian.* Chester, Connecticut: Globe Pequot Press, 1978.

Willard, Everett, quoted in *Proud Tradition, Pure Vermont Maple.* Charlotte, VT: Perceptions, Inc., 1981. Videocassette.

Williams, Samuel. *The Natural and Civil History of Vermont.* Middlebury, VT: Mills and White. 1809.

Wiseman, Frederick. "Abenaki." *The Vermont Encyclopedia.* Edited by John J. Duffy, Samuel B. Hand, and Ralph H. Orth. Hanover, NH: University Press of New England, 2003.

About the Author

Betty Ann Lockhart and her photographer/videographer husband, Don, live in a two-hundred-year-old brick farmhouse in Vermont—a station on the Underground Railroad. One ancient sugar maple graces the dooryard, and three wooly sheep reign over the barn.

A graduate of the State University of New York at Cortland and Hofstra University, Betty Ann taught in the College of Education at the University of Vermont until she and her husband began their educational video production company, Perceptions, Inc. Their three videos about Vermont maple have been honored with national and international awards, and were selected to represent the United States at foreign film festivals. They are recipients of an award from the Vermont Maple Industry Council in appreciation for their maple video production, and also the President's Award from the Vermont Maple Sugarmakers' Association and the Vermont Maple Industry Council. They were named the Vermont Maple Persons of the Year by the Vermont Maple Industry Council.

Betty Ann is a member of the Vermont Maple History Committee and the Center for Research on Vermont at the University of Vermont. She also serves as a trustee of the Vermont Maple Festival, and is a member of the board of the Vermont Maple Foundation. She is a member of the Vermont Maple Sugarmakers' Association and Chittenden County, Addison County and Rutland County Sugarmakers' Associations. Betty

ABOUT THE AUTHOR

Ann also serves as secretary of the Charlotte Land Trust and the Historic Quinlan Schoolhouse Board of Directors. She has authored *The Maple Sugaring Story—A Guide for Teaching and Learning About the Maple Industry* and several pamphlets.

Betty Ann has frequently stated that Vermont sugarmakers are among the finest, smartest people she has ever met!